Live Java

—Database to Cyberspace—

Live Java

—Database to Cyberspace—

David Levine

AP PROFESSIONAL

AP Professional is a Division of Academic Press, Inc.

Boston   San Diego   New York
London   Sydney   Tokyo   Toronto

AP PROFESSIONAL

An Imprint of ACADEMIC PRESS, INC.
A Division of HARCOURT BRACE & COMPANY

ORDERS (USA and Canada): 1-800-3131-APP or APP@ACAD.COM
AP Professional Orders: 6277 Sea Harbor Dr., Orlando, FL 32821-9816

Europe/Middle East/Africa: 0-11-44 (0) 181-300-3322
Orders: AP Professional 24-28 Oval Rd., London NW1 7DX

Japan/Korea: 03-3234-3911-5
Orders: Harcourt Brace Japan, Inc., Ichibancho Central Building 22-1, Ichibancho Chiyoda-Ku, Tokyo 102

Australia: 02-517-8999
Orders: Harcourt Brace & Co. Australia, Locked Bag 16, Marrickville, NSW 2204 Australia

Other International: (407) 345-3800
AP Professional Orders: 6277 Sea Harbor Dr., Orlando FL 32821-9816

Editorial: 1300 Boylston St., Chestnut Hill, MA 02167 (617)232-0500

Web: http://www.apnet.com/approfessional

United Kingdom Edition published by
ACADEMIC PRESS LIMITED
24–28 Oval Road, London NW1 7DX

Levine, David. 1966-
      Live Java: Database to Cyberspace / David Levine.
             p.   cm.
      Includes bibliographical references and index.
      ISBN 0-12-445485-2
      1. Java (Computer program language) I. Title.
   QA76.73.J38L48 1996
   005.2—dc20
                                                                                96-23412
                                                                                CIP

Printed in the United States of America
 96 97 98 99   IP   9 8 7 6 5 4 3 2 1

Contents

Contents

Acknowledgments

This book was written interactively, or Socratically, on the HuskyLabs' MOO (Multiuser Object Oriented) environment. When I ran into a block, I'd pose a question to Sick (Michael Reece), Obvious (Dave Carter) or Mozart (Matthew Ross Davis), then cut and paste the ensuing discussion into a text editor, and refine it for the book. Their background in C, C++, PERL, MOO, Lingo, HyperTalk and various media formats was indispensable as a foundation for the book. As the lead developer of MoonBean, Mike's heroic coding figures prominently in Immersive Java. Fluent Java is based on a tutorial Matt and I gave at Internet World, Fall 1995. Dave Carter is responsible for a lot of the MOO code and explanations of Object theory.

Besides designing the book cover, Monica Larson (a.k.a. sceptical, because of her limited faith in MOO as an effective business communication tool. She thought we'd just be playing.) contributed an overall vision of simplicity and elegance in interface design that generally precluded the use of Java on our Web sites unless it was necessary. Most important, Monica took care of me and The Bean (our daughter, Zoe) while I obsessed on this book.

Blaine Pennington took the pretty pictures on the back of the book and scattered liberally throughout the Web site.

Doug Birdzell also deserves thanks for his elaborate PERL constructs that form the foundation of our electronic retailing operations, now being ported to Java/NEO/Joe.

Ruth Fellingham (nomad) held things together at the office, while I neglected the business to write this book.

Mark Conway Wirt and Carl Hillsman of Intrepid Network Technologies provided invaluable support on Internet administration and database engineering.

Our friends at UUcom, particularly Curtis Generous and Rick Dunbar, have taught us an awful lot about systems and network management and provided the essential support that has allowed us to venture off and explore new terrain in application development and design.

Thanks also to business allies like John Griebling at MFS Datanet; Tom Patterson, Electronic Commerce Guru, Mark Bentley, and the rest of the VIRTUE team; Jamie Clark, Stephen Balbach, and Stephen Schwing at ClarkNet; Dixon Doll at Oracle, Howard Gordon at Xing Technologies, and Dale Olson at Silicon Graphics.

Steve Shapero (socks), Big Jim Lentini, John Berndt, Ken Karpay, Kurt Kolb, Fletcher, Adnan Schaben, Rachel Schwartz, Dave Balcom, Chris Jacobs, and Jerry Jacobs helped get HuskyLabs off the ground, along with Bob Rytter, Pam Jacobs, and Gail Boren at Rytter's, Victor Hoskins at the State of Maryland, and the rest of the high-tech Hamden Crew.

Chris Spina of Sun Microsystems, who sold me my first SPARCstation, is partially to blame for my current hardware addiction. Bob Demartino, Lisa Bunyon, Ed Peri, David Showalter, Mike Winkler, Craig Anderson, and the rest of SMCC have been a blast to work with. Sun has a mighty bright future thanks to them.

Most of all, thanks goes out to my clients, customers, and associates, for whom this book is really written. In particular Edwin Warfield IV and Glenn Ferber @Review.Net; Marshall Nichols at The National Petroleum Council; Richard Riemann of AudioCenter; Lois Phillips at BellSouth; Bill McBride and Bill Hamilton at Holland & Knight; Jothan Adler and The Adler Group; Larry Kessner and Hilary Schneider at The Baltimore Sun; Chuck Lyons at The Gazette; Adam Lilling and Jotham Schwartz of Pentagon CDs and Tapes; everyone at National Public Radio (particularly Rich Dean); Dr. Abraham Wagner, Yukie Novick, Morris Levine, Rebecca King, Patrick Chang and various other quasi-governmental operatives; the folks at the National Telecommunications Infrastructure Agency (particularly Brian Harris and Steve Saleh); Bruce Ross-Davis, my old boss; Steve Hull and Karl Eisenhower at PoliticsNow; Julie Hansen, Stephanie Rosenberg and Colin Maloney at PenguinUSA; Michael Rau at Radio Data Group; Dennis Dunbar of Wireless Data Systems; Robert Barnhill, Jerry Garland and Pat Sweeney at Tessco; Sharon Hewlett and Maureen McManus at Struever Bros. Eccles & Rouse, Inc.; Steve Pospisil of The Rouse Company; Jake Oliver of The AfroAmerican Newspapers; Chuck Lyons at The Gazette; Seth McMillan, Leslie Leven, Richard Granat, Bill Hamilton, Neal Friedman, Susan Sacks, and many others provided opportunities to test out new techologies and invaluable guidance and support.

Jenifer Niles, Jacqueline Young, and Barbara Northcott at AP Professional/Harcourt Brace, thanks for your patience and perseverence.

Hello to all our friends and neighbors in Shepherdstown, WV. (Particularly Kendra, Bradley Sanders, Lissa & Garth, the Kings, and everyone who smiles and says "hi.")

Of course, big thanks to Jane & Blaine, Dan, Mom & Dad, Nana, The Long Island Levines, The Donnenbergs (and Mulligans), The Larsons (and Soderstroms), The Heymans, The Levinsons, and the rest of the extended clan.

And thank you for reading this book.s

Foreword

Approximately once every decade there is a spark in the computing industry that catapults an entire community of engineers, educators, managers, and users into a new evolution of the computing experience. We are now in such a stage of computing evolution, commonly referred to as network-centric computing.

"Net-centric" computing is a concept in which the individual user accesses a "virtual system" that comprises various resources that are distributed throughout an organization. These resources exist in cyberspace somewhere in the form of downloadable applications, content, information, and data. In other words, in a net-centric computing environment, the network itself takes on many attributes of the computer. The network is the computer. And the resources of cyberspace are like one huge disk drive.

This net-centric model makes it possible for unlimited user experience. Thus, a revolution and demand for access regardless of a particular operating system, regardless of a particular vendor's hardware, software, or communication protocols, and regardless of geographical, political, social, or economic constraints. The content is also unlimited and diverse.

David Levine's *Live Java* has addressed the technology which will launch new computing solutions well into the next decade. The book addresses the issues we are all now faced with:

- Building an Internet/Intranet strategy.
- Addressing the high recurring cost of system management.
- The need for improved data security and integrity.
- Producing product innovation for business advantages.
- Distributed applications and data across heterogeneous platforms.
- What these new concepts are and how they differ from the old.

Live Java will be enormously beneficial for people who also need to address the non–programming language issues surrounding Java with respect to: "What is Java?" and "What do I do with it?" as well as "How do I implement it?"

Finally, let me articulate the significance of Java by stating that it is the Lego of computing. Lego blocks are the most ingenious toy in the world, and have not lost their appeal after decades on the market. Why? They are easy to assemble. Even though parts are different, they all fit together. They are also reliable and unbreakable. I can't ever remember seeing a broken Lego block. The best thing about them was that from Lego blocks you could construct any object. The type of object was limited only by imagination. The objects could be small and discrete or large and multidimensional. What else could one ask of a product or of a programming language environment?

Kirk Brown

Tactical Engineer
Internet/Intranet Business Solutions
Sun Microsystems, Inc.

Preamble

If you've picked this book off the shelf, you've in some way, shape or form been touched by the Java HypeMachine. I have no doubt that in your life you will be touched by Java itself and its capabilities. As you're considering whether or not to buy this book, or if you've already bought it and are considering whether to read it cover to cover or skip around for tidbits of code, I thought I'd let you know up front my intentions in writing this book, what it covers, and my secret design to indoctrinate the reader into the Java cult. My intention is to change the way you work, think, and live. How you will be affected will depend on your background. I will state very clearly that Java will affect the way you communicate, the way you approach problems, and the way you solve them. If you do not wish to participate in the Java revolution, this will be a good time to close this book.

Structure of this Book

Live Java is divided into four sections:

1. **Revolutionary Java**
    This section contains a historical overview that leads to an understanding of Java's emergence and significance in publishing and communications. It distinguishes Java from other programming languages and provides some direction for its implementation. It is important to understand how to approach Java development strategically, in the context of the Internet and the corporate intranet. This section is geared toward the non-technical reader who will need to understand Java in the context of business, computers, and the media.

2. **Fluent Java**
    This is the hands-on section for nascent Java programmers. The reader will capture and dissect an applet, and learn to create new ones. No previous experience necessary.

3. **Tactical Java**
    The section for corporate Information Systems (IS) staff, consultants, integrators, and management. Strategies for deploying Network Computers (NCs), database access, and custom application development.

4. **Immersive Java**
    Advanced application development with a focus: what it tales to actually build a useful project in Java. Not something to "spice up a page," but to add real capabilities that were previously unavailable to networked computers. Provides source code to MoonBean, a multiuser, multipurpose conferencing, and collaboration system.

Supporting Web Site, Mailing List, and Laboratory

For this book, we've developed a Web site with source code, applets for your use, and pointers to important Java resources. As new uses for Java emerge, and specifications change, you will receive updated information. It is significant that there is no CD-ROM in this book. All the source code and software you will need to take advantage of *Live Java* is available to readers through links from:

```
http://www.lab.com/LiveJava/
```

Some of the materials on the site are restricted to readers of this book. You will need to provide the following:

```
Username: Java
```

```
Password: NEOJoe
```

One of Java's best features is its ability to create applications that inhabit networks. It would seem a little silly to lock the software in a CD-ROM and distribute it that way. By the time you load it, it could be outdated. By distributing the software on the Net, we can keep it updated. At the *Live Java* site, you can also sign up for our mailing list and create a persona on our live, java-based interactive developer's environment, The Lab.

Whenever you see a URL:

http://www.lab.com/LiveJava/

it means that a graphic, chart, applet, or source code is available on the Live Java Web site.

Live Java requires reader participation. Most of the experiments can be performed with the latest version of Netscape, available from **http://www.netscape.com**, or HotJava on a platform that supports Java, such as Win95, NT, XWindows or MacOS, and the Java Developer's Kit (JDK) available from **http://www.javasoft.com**. A direct TCP/IP connection to the Internet is also required, as described in the hands-on section of **Fluent Java**, below.

I. Revolutionary Java

"The Killer Application of the 90s is People"

—*Pavel Curtis*

## CHAPTER 1

The Java Manifesto

What is Java?

Java is a programming language.

Java is not:

- an application
- a protocol
- an operating system

As a programming language, it can be used to write applications, protocols and even operating systems.

Why is this programming language different from all other programming languages?

Java is not significantly different, syntactically. In fact, it has intentionally retained features of other programming languages such as C and

C++. This makes it easy for people who already know how to program to move their applications to Java. Java has been called C++--.

The key to Java's success is that it was designed for today's computing environment: lots of very different types of machines connected by a network. It is also designed for tomorrow's computing environment, where devices that are closer to today's consumer electronics or appliances can receive and deliver data and software through an almost ubiquitous, heterogeneous cyberspace. Any current or future device can be connected to and participate in this cyberspace if it supports the Java Virtual Machine (JVM) specification.

The Java Virtual Machine

The designers of Java understood the mechanics of this cyberspace and took the first step toward creating it: the Java Virtual Machine. With Java, you can write a program that will run in cyberspace, regardless of the device that is connected. This is because you are writing software for an imaginary device, rather than a real one. The producers of current and future hardware and the software that runs exclusively on these proprietary devices have the blueprints for this imaginary device and can either etch the run-time component of the Java Virtual Machine in the silicon or produce a software buffer that will allow the Java program come to life and inhabit the part of cyberspace maintained by that physical device.

Emerging from the Primordial Web

It might seem dubious to declare the World Wide Web obsolete. It's only a few years old and has become a quite popular institution. But the fact is, the Web browser alone cannot continue to develop as the complete desktop document retrieval, multimedia player and communications tool for the enterprise network and the public Internet. It will be instructive to view the development of the Internet and its unification behind the Web, look at how this system ceased to "scale," or expand comfortably, and then see how Java returned us to a more flexible Internet while improving the ease of use even beyond that afforded by the Web browser.

To explain the significance and understand the utility of Java, I have had to rely on metaphors: political, theological and scientific. This is to avoid computer-industry jargon so that Java can speak directly to all the people beyond the industry who will be touched by it. It is also because Java, as an embodiment of the Net, will affect our life and culture beyond its role as a useful tool for programmers currently coding in C and C++.

A Declaration of Independence from the HyperText Transfer Protocol

There comes a time in the life cycle of every civilization when a capability arises that is so useful and solves so many problems that an new age is born. For early man, there were the Stone Age and the Iron Age, based on new technological innovations. For example, clay pots changed nomadic society to domestic society because food could be stored. The Industrial Age moved us from an agrarian/mercantile society to where we are today, a state known to critics and scholars as Late Capitalism. Many of these thinkers are describing the next stage as the Digital Age and seeing signs of its imminent birth in our postindustrial economy.

These are certainly revolutionary times, and in our accelerated culture, the technologies that seem to be the revolutionary ones are often trampled by progress themselves. But in their death, they give birth to new capabilities. It will be instructive to take a quick look at how the Internet emerged from the military/industrial/scientific complex onto

Main Street and Wall Street as a mass-market phenomenon before it hit a wall, unable to deliver to this market the potential of cyberspace promised by the media. The key to the life cycle of the Net is that it was developed as a communications systems, but was co-opted as a publishing platform. By the time the Net became the Web, an easy-to-use, commercially viable product, it was a stitched-together interface to many different communications protocols, file formats, and presentation methods.

The Web was a victim of its own success. It seemed so useful, with information spread across the globe interlocked in hypertext references. Indexed in mammoth search engines. As it gained in popularity the authority over its development moved from the academic and scientific standards bodies to powerful corporate concerns. In either case, whether the standards were guarded by a task force, a working group or by a corporation, the ability to innovate was not in the hands of the Internet users and Web developers. The software giants dictated the formats that content could be produced in and the protocols that could be used to deliver that content. Internet users and producers would have to sit back and wait for the next release of a piece of software to add capabilities to or improve functionality on their Web site. With Java, the software is delivered by the site producer or developer directly to the user when the Web site is contacted.

## CHAPTER 2

The Internet and the Web

Internets before the Web

The Internet was built for communications between computers and, by extension, the users sitting at those computers. When a need arose, a capability was developed, the solution implemented, and a standard agreed upon through the issuing and discussion of an RFC (Request for Comments).

Generally, a protocol (the syntax and data format and data type used by the computers to accept exchanges of information packets) was developed to handle a particular type of message. When a new protocol was developed, software had to be written for each computer that participated in the messaging process. For example:

- SMTP (Simple Mail Transfer Protocol) and POP (Post Office Protocol) were developed for passing messages between computers.
- Telnet was developed for remote logins, to launch applications on remote computers, talk with other users, access data, and read files.

- FTP (File Transfer Protocol) was developed to move text, binary files and applications between computers on a network.
- NNTP (Network News Transfer Protocol) was developed to facilitate discussions between multiple parties on the Internet, threading those discussions by topics and subtopics.

Each protocol necessitated the development of a compliant software package for each computer platform that needed to send and receive messages, serve or collect data, accept or make connections. This worked fine for the sophisticated audience of early Internet users, but when complete suites of Internet communications applications began showing up on corporate desktops, for use within the corporate computing environment, users were often overwhelmed by the capabilities. They did not know which software was appropriate for which task, or what feature or configuration of any particular piece of software was the right one to select. Managing a corporate network became increasingly complex, and support costs skyrocketed. The Web browser was the easiest, most functional piece of software in this package, so people wanted it to do everything. The only option was to extend the browser to handle all these functions, which created a new, very complex and difficult to manage application environment. What was specific and dedicated to navigate and explore deta has become monolithic.

Java suggests a solution to this: distribute highly tailored software designed for a particular task from a central computer when the particular service that requires the software is requested. Upgrades can be distributed from that computer, too. Different users can be provisioned with software packages geared toward a particular task, to access a certain subset of data or input certain types of responses.

Freeing the Net from the Web

The success of the Web is partly my fault. I was one of the early entrepreneurs who hit the streets and the lecture circuits with nothing but a laptop and a browser, explaining to corporate managers, marketers, and publishers that the Web was a vast new marketplace, where all they would have to do was reconstruct their content in HyperText Markup Language (HTML), load it on a server and watch the world come to their door.

The enemy at the time was the online services, which kept their audiences locked into a "proprietary" platform with canned content, very limited access to the Net through gateways, and hordes of people typing gibberish in chats and forums. As Web proselytizers, we told them they should publish on the Web, and, that eventually, the online services would be nothing but one more path to the Web. The Web was the future, where any information could be located and accessed with the click of a mouse. The Internet would be as easy to use as, if not easier to use than, the online services the Web would make obsolete.

But as the Internet became the World Wide Web, with slick graphics, animations, sounds, video and search engines, a very key component of the Internet was lost. That was real-time, live human interaction. It was as if the small towns, the quaint eateries, the juke-joints, cafes and pubs had been bulldozed and replaced with strip malls and 7-11s.

It's not that the backwater hangouts ceased to exist, it's that new users weren't being given the tools to inhabit them. Rather than deliver a full suite of Internet applications to every user, a standard package for Web browsing and e-mail was delivered. At first, this was two separate pieces, such as the one from Netscape called the Personal Edition, consisting of a browser (Netscape Navigator) for viewing Web documents and an e-mail program (Eudora) for sending and receiving mail through POPmail. Internet Service Providers (ISPs) were having such a good time selling SLIP (Serial Line Internet Protocol) and PPP (Point to Point Protocol) to meet the demand for the Web access, many stopped selling, or charged a premium on, UNIX shell accounts that were necessary for many forms of real-time communication. Some considered it a security risk to let users log into the computers through a Terminal Emulation program (such as Telnet). With Netscape 2.0, a single piece of software was all the user would need to send and receive mail, browse the Web and read USENET news. The browser could be extended through plug-ins and helper applications, but these were not geared toward real-time interactive communities. These live human communities were buried deeper and deeper beneath the new types of graphics, media formats for audio and video, layout capabilities and animations.

## CHAPTER 3

The Death of Multimedia.
The Birth of the Medium.

Before networks, computers were not useful communications tools. They could compose documents, but then would have to go "out of band" (to a printer or a disk and then to a fax machine or the post office) to deliver the document. They could produce applications, but would have to go out of band to a shrinkwrapped box and then a store shelf to have the application delivered. With the advent of network-centric computing, the machine that produces a document can transfer the document to another computer, which can then deliver the documents to other computers on the network. The same thing happens with applications. A programmer writes a program, compiles it for a particular platform, loads it onto a server across the network, and lets other users download the software and install it on their system. This software can then be used for various communications chores.

Before Java, the work of the clients and servers across the Internet was not very balanced. There were essentially three scenarios for networked computing on the Internet:

1. **Terminal**: the client computer provides little more than a window to the activity taking place on the server computer. The server

computer needs to be able to multitask and handle a high load from all the people working on it.

2. **The Thin Client**: a piece of software is good for one particular thing, but a whole suite of them is needed to get any real work done on the Internet. You have one client to transfer files (FTP), one client to login remotely (Telnet), one client to browse the Web, one client to read news and one client for e-mail. With the advent of the Web browser, a whole suite of "helper applications" needed to be introduced to display different forms of data: video clips, sounds, graphics, advanced page layout and 3-D models. In this case, the Web browser needed to understand a few things: how to access a Uniform Resource Location (URL), how to present information described with HTML and how to pass other file types to helper applications.

3. **The Extended Browser**: the client software initiates a connection and retrieves data using the protocol indicated by the URL. Many types of data and protocols are are handled internally by the browser. The Web browser becomes an application platform, almost an extended desktop-to-network operating system, by having the capability to handle different protocols and different types of data and display them within the browser window. Building in protocol handlers for news, mail, file transfers, and the Web creates a bloated, unwieldy browser. A Web interface is not always the best way to read mail or news.

Even using a browser for its designated task, browsing the Web, becomes complicated as content developers attempt to push the HyperText Transfer Protocol (HTTP) session to be an advanced multimedia distribution platform. Distributing a new type of file using a new protocol, such as RealAudio's streaming sound and Xing's low bit rate video, requires setting a MIME-type. MIME (Multipurpose Internet Mail Extension) was developed as a way to deliver nontext files in Internet mail without uuencoding them. (Uuencoding stands for UNIX-to-UNIX encoding, which converts the binary files to an ASCII document. At the receiving end, the binary must be uudecoded before it can be viewed, played or read.) This allowed users to easily attach graphics, sounds, or formatted text to e-mail, and be reasonably assured that the user on the other end would be able to use the file. MIME became a method for negotiating the format in which the server should send to the browser.

The Web server software at HuskyLabs defines 57 different MIME.types in its configuration file. Here are a few:

```
type=application/octet-stream   exts=bin,exe
type=audio/basic                exts=au,snd
type=audio/x-pn-realaudio       exts=ra,ram
type=image/jpeg                 exts=jpeg,jpg,jpe
type=text/html                  exts=htm,html
type=video/quicktime            exts=qt,mov
type=magnus-internal/imagemap   exts=map
# perl applications
type=application/x-httpd-cgi    exts=pl
# V R M L
type=x-world/x-vrml             exts=wrl
```

The first column describes the general type of the content and then the subtype; the second column denotes the extension of the file (the few letters after the dot in the file name).

Just as the MIME-type informs the server how to deliver the file, the .mailcap file lets the client know how to display it. Once the document or file arrived, the browser would either need to know how to handle all the different file formats included in the document or would need to hand these off to helper applications. When a user approaches a site that has advanced multimedia functions, that user would have to beef up the browser with plug-ins to display or launch the files or applications within the browser frame or have collected in advance and preconfigured the various applications. This leaves very little room to be surprised by a new capability. More likely, users will

be disappointed that they reached a site unprepared. Under UNIX, the
.mailcap file looks like this:

```
# plays AIFF files
audio/x-aiff; sfplay %s
# use this to play MPEG audio if you have maplay
    installed
audio/x-mpeg; maplay -; stream-buffer-size=2000

# use for MPEG video files if mpeg_play is installed
video/mpeg; mpeg_play %s
# this is the default for non GIF or JPEG images
image/*; xv %s
# for an external viewer for GIF and JPEG images
# uncomment for XV to act as your external viewer.
# image/gif; xv %s
# image/jpg; xv %s
```

A mailcap file is how, under UNIX and XWindows, the browser
knows what helper application to launch, or that it should attempt to
handle the incoming files itself (which is the default if nothing is specified). In other operating systems, there is a dialog box that creates
what is essentially a mailcap file. In this example, the first item in a
line represents the SubGroup (application, audio file, image, video
file, etc.) and the second is the item (gif, mpeg, etc.) as SubGroup/
Item. Beyond the semicolon (;) is the application that will be
launched to handle, present or play the file. If the item is an asterisk
(*) or wildcard, it means that any image file (tiff, ras, etc.) would be
sent to the application xv (Xviewer) if it is not a type that is handled
in-line by the browser. The comments in the mailcap file indicate that
if you specify an item and a helper application to be used, it will override the fact that the browser is perfectly capable of handling the
image in-line.

## CHAPTER 4

Plug in, Turn On, Drop Out

Retaining Control over Presentation

A problem with counting on media formats to launch helper applications is that the author loses control over the frame. When you don't know where these are going to launch on the screen, context control is difficult. For example, the MIME-types/mailcap/helper-application paradigm won't enable you to build a video into your page with subtitles or other annotations in HTML. Netscape created their plug-ins to address this problem.

Plug-ins are essentially a client-side API (applied programming interface) that allows software developers to write new applications in C or C++ for a particular platform so that Web producers can take advantage of the software within the browser's frame. When a MIME-type is encountered that fits a plug-in on the users system, an in-line plug-in is launched rather than an outside-the-browser helper application. The trouble is that plug-ins are available unevenly for various platforms. Generally, a PC plug-in is available first, a Macintosh later, and a UNIX will be released eventually, if at all. Even if you're on one of the more popular platforms, with the proliferation of plug-ins, you will be constantly encountering sites that will be ineffectual if you don't have the right plug-in. As new applications are developed, content will need to be produced in new proprietary formats to utilize the new capabilities. The nice thing about the Web in the early days was that you had few choices. If you marked up your text in HTML and added a few graphics in the GIF format, you knew that users would be able to get the information you were offering. (There was even some well-reasoned opposition early on to the concept of adding graphic formats such as GIF to the Web browser, the capability that made Mosaic a mass-market phenomenon. When we explore the intentions of HTML, you'll understand why.)

Netscape as the Microsoft of the 90s

When a browser hits a Web server, it leaves an impression. If you sit behind the Webserver, you can read these impressions, or logs. There is a certain amount of information passed to the server by the browser when it exchanges handshakes and agrees to transfer files. The browser declares the host it came from (by IP address, which can then be translated into a host name on a particular network), the computing platform (or operating system), and thebBrowser type and version. Examining the access logs on the HuskyLabs server shows that Internet surfers are exploring with at least 21 different browsers, including:

- Arena
- Cello
- CERN-LineMode
- Charlotte
- Chimera
- Emissary
- MacWeb
- Microsoft Internet Explorer

- Emacs-w3
- Lynx
- Mosaic for Amiga
- NetCruiser
- Netscape
- Netsurfer
- NCSA Mosaic
- OmniWeb
- Spry Air Mosaic
- Frontier Technologies Internet Browser.

With all these browsers cruising the Web, can you comfortably develop for Netscape? Why would anyone use the CERN LineMode browser nowadays? How was Netscape able to set the production standards? How does this lead us to the significance of Java?

The answer to these questions lies in the foundations of HTML and the Web. Let's look at the second question first. Why would anyone use the CERN LineMode browser? Probably because they want information, want it in HTML form, and don't want to have to take their hands off the keyboards and reach for the mouse while they're browsing. HTML is a "SGML DTD," which in English means it is a Document Type Definition of the Standard Generalized Markup Language. In plainer English, it means that it is intended for describing the parts of the document (the title, the headings, the body text) rather than specifying how the parts of the document look (color, point size, font). Thus, the document can be presented to the reader in many different ways, according to the reader's preferences and equipment. I might want all the headers to be in a different color than the body text but the same size because I am using the CERN LineMode browser in a terminal interface that cannot set point sizes or even show bold. They key to HTML is its functionality as a way to share information (documents) with a diverse population of users across a network. If you try to control the end user's experience too much, you lose that functionality.

HTML is thus a platform-independent and device-independent means of distributing and presenting documents, and in a very similar way Java is a platform- and device-independent way to distribute and run applications. HTML and HTTP, the two primary components of the Web, were developed at CERN particle physics laboratory as a way to organize and share data generated in the collision of atomic particles. It was not for entertainment or mass media. It did not have to survive in a competitive marketplace, it just had to meet a need, and it met that need very well.

Netscape, on the other hand, was a business. It had to take a free, open specification and produce it in such a way as to develop a faithful following of publishers and surfers and distinguish itself from the competition. HTML was not robust enough to provide the gee-whiz factor for mass-market consumption or professional publishing. Designers wanted to specify background colors, point sizes, columns, margins and fonts. The official World Wide Web working group was addressing these issues but reluctant to move the display control from the user to the publisher. It was against the underlying principle of SGML, that the codes should specify parts of the document so that different displays could handle them according to the needs of the user or requirements of output device.

So Netscape made the decision to publish their own extensions to HTML, beginning the move to "Netscape Enhanced" pages. But publishers who took advantage of the advanced features, such as tables and colors, could no longer count on surfers to get all the features on the page. For example, if the information was complex and required tabulation for the best presentation, the content could wind up unintelligible in non-Netscape browsers, as one long column of numbers rather than a matrix. Publishers had to consider both the best presentation and the lowest common denominator, sometimes leading to solutions like the "browser recognizer" Common Gateway Interface (CGI) program, that read from the header information on the browser's request what type of browser the request was issued by and delivered content in the best format for that browser. In many ways this was a reversion to the early days of the Web, when server administrators would load the same content into gopher servers and Web servers to provide for users of both protocols.

For publishers, the only possible solution to the situation was for a company like Netscape to win the war against the standards bodies and populate the world's desktops. "Formatted for Netscape" and "Netscape Now!" began to appear on most format-rich sites. Netscape was becoming the Microsoft of the Internet, quickly gaining the market share and the mind share and turning that into a powerful control mechanism: owning the desktop API of the Web. Its codeword was Live. Live3D (for inline Virtual Worlds), LiveMedia (for inline desktop conferencing and media streaming), and LiveWire (for Netsite server connectivity with databases) were all part of its Live Objects approach. (Netscape's scripting language was called LiveScript before Sun Microsystems and Netscape agreed to codevelop and copromote it as JavaScript). Netscape would become an application platform where Live Objects from around the Internet could find a home, regardless of their origin.

It seemed like a great approach. Let all the little software developers develop for Netscape, the browser/application platform with the almost limitless distribution, rather than Microsoft, the operating system with the wide distribution, that ran the browser. While both companies would provide software for the Internet user, Netscape would control the customer. Netscape was way out ahead technology-wise, building in so many capabilities, so quickly, that the other browsers didn't stand a chance. The strategy seemed perfect, until Java.

With Java, the other browsers didn't have to play catch-up on so many fronts. They didn't have to provide a plug-in API. They didn't have to provide frames. They didn't have to develop new services, new user interfaces or new capabilities. They could let those arrive with the content. But we're getting ahead of ourselves. To understand the power of Java in the marketplace, we should take a look at Microsoft.

Microsoft as the AOL of the 90s

Meanwhile, Microsoft was also striving to be the Microsoft of the Internet. It saw in its legions of programmers trained in Visual Basic and OLE (Object Linking and Embedding) an army of developers who would produce advanced multimedia publications using a proprietary format codenamed Blackbird. In an ever-shifting strategy, Microsoft hoped to dominate the online and Internet world by offering newspapers spiced with inline MPEG and AVI video streams, scrolling text marquees, flashy animations and advanced layout capabilities. It would bundle its browser, Microsoft Internet Explorer, in with its operating system, which would connect by default to its online service where users would encounter publications enhanced with Blackbird tags. Information on your favorite stocks would automagically, using OLE, be opened in Excel. Photographs would rotate on the page, and selecting one would open a new multimedia adventure.

Sure, there would be links to the Internet, and anyone could venture out into the World Wide Web, but once they got there, they would be stuck in an expanse of flat, static documents. Major publications would launch on Microsoft's proprietary online service to take advantage of the new capabilities, and sites out on the Internet would start to adopt those capabilities, driving demand for Microsoft authoring tools, Microsoft browsers and Microsoft servers. If it wasn't for those meddling kids from Sun.

Microsoft is now straddling the line. It has licensed Java for inclusion in future versions of its Windows operating systems, and brought OLE, OCX (OLE Controls), Visual Basic, Blackbird and Java together under the ActiveX banner. It is possible that as developers move from Visual Basic to Java, Microsoft will lose its dominance of the desktop API and become just another software company, particularly if the Network Computer (NC) running the JVM unseats the Personal Computer (PC) as the desktop device of choice on corporate networks.

AOL as the Netscape of the 90s

But we're getting ahead of ourselves in the story. Java has not yet been introduced. As far as the public and the industry is concerned, the Internet battle is not between competing platforms, programming languages and browsers but between the Internet and online services. Without having half the capabilities of the online services, the Web still posed an enormous threat to their success. As a publishing platform, the Web blew the cap off the online Petri dish. What was once contained as a medium for a captive audience was now in the public domain. The teeming millions who logged onto America Online (AOL) every day and had been content to read clippings from *Business Week* or *Time*, chat with friends in various forums, write email and gave access to the Internet through limited gopher and FTP gateways were now clamoring for the Web. There was a race among online services to deliver the Web, even though they would be losing ad dollars by letting their users peek through the curtains of the theatre out into the world. In a revenue-sharing arrangement, AOL pays money to a content provider based on how long a user stays in their "area." This time-based model is very different from a Web site's advertising model, which is based on "page hits," "page impressions" or "exposures," one full download of a page of text and graphics.

AOL realized that if they became just another dumb pipe to the Web, a utility, they would not survive. The Internet access business is a low-margin one. As far as profit on dial-up, AOL makes a lot more money on all the people who pay the $9.95/mo base fee and don't use all the free hours than the ones who stay on for a long time and pay for more hours. People who stay on surfing the Web would cut into the advertising margins, as advertisers support AOL's proprietary content. Trying to get users to search back issues of *Business Week* when there were massive archives of source documents out on the Web was not a long-term strategy, so AOL added to its strength: community, rather than content. AOL had something the Web didn't have: real time interaction. Chats. Auditoriums. Celebrity guests. Publishers had the content, but

AOL had the people. If the people were interacting and producing their own content in real-time, who needed the publishers? AOL would produce its own wacky characters and scenarios, a live user-interactive soap opera. It started the greenhouse project to encourage its users to make money online and make money for AOL. Compared to the brain-dead interactivity offered by the Web, with its forms interface, CGI scripts, and client pulls, AOL was as close to live as the Net could get.

Speaking of live, it seems like we've come full circle. All of a sudden AOL realizes it had something all along that the Web did not. It had a platform that supported instant innovation, live content. It is way ahead of Netscape and the Web in terms of interactivity, tightly linked applications, user interface and communications capabilities. It didn't need all those big-shot content providers, as it had its community members, who loved listening to each other, fighting with each other, flirting with each other. It realized that it had something that people would not give up for the Web. Until Java came along, the jig was up. All of a sudden, every Web site could be an online service, or better, a community of people who had a good reason to be together. At least a better reason than the fact that they received a disk with "10 FREE HOURS" on it.

Live, text-based human communities, built on MUDs (Multi-User Dungeons or Dimensions), MOOs (MUDs Object Oriented) or IRC (Internet Relay Chat) channels, similar to the ones on online systems, often more complex than those, lived in the Internet but required some type of terminal interface or special client software to access them. The Web could not provide direct access to these worlds but could point to them by location (URL). When users came upon a reference to an interactive environment in a Web page, they selected a link to a telnet URL (such as telnet://lambda.parc.xerox.com:8888), and got an "application not found" error if they had not preconfigured the PC to launch a telnet application when the protocol was announced. Because of the ubiquitous nature of the Web browser, Web content producers implemented very ineffective "bulletin boards" or posting services where users could fill out a form and submit it to the server.

It was then almost instantly made available to other browsers hitting the server. These types of threaded discussions lacked the intimacy that was created by the effect of spending real time in an environment that could not be created by the "getting" and "putting" of the Hyper-Text Transfer Protocol. It did not create the sensation that two creatures were inhabiting the same environment. Often, the pseudoconversations would degenerate into; "Bob!! you still there????" "Where'd you go???" "I'll be back in 10 minutes!!" These messages would be preserved for relative posterity, available to the casual Net surfer. Besides lacking a sense of real-time communion, there is little privacy on the Web. In fact, if you go to a powerful search engine and look for your own name, you'll probably see scraps of public conversations on newsgroups and mailing lists archived as an embarrassing reminder of a particularly heated discussion that quickly lost relevance. The importance of maintaining the distinction between real-time interaction (worlds), group discussions (lists) and publications (Web sites) becomes painfully clear.

Before the advent of Java, seemlessly integrating real-time communications into a Web site was not possible. HTTP simply did not support it, and using other protocols besides HTTP, by definition, required applications that were not natively a part of the Web. The only options were to provide a link that would launch a Telnet session for remote login to the multiuser world or to provide a "helper application" that provides some of the basic graphical elements. This application had to be developed for each platform and distributed in advance to users, just as with any other type of content handler that extended HTML beyond the basic MIME-types. When Prospero Systems introduced their Global Chat software, billing it as the first Web-integrated real-time chat program, there was an outcry on technical lists from people who had been using the same technology, Internet Relay Chat, for almost a decade. Prospero had taken a program, distributed freely over the Internet, built a graphical interface that could be launched as a helper application by defining the "chat" MIME-type and extension, and announced it as a new technology. This demonstrates how stifled the ability to innovate on the Internet had become.

CHAPTER 5

If Java Is the Answer, What Is the Question?

Everyone on the Net had the same questions at the same time:

- "How do we provide interactivity on our Web site?"
- "How do we easily create advanced applications that will run on all the different Internet-connected computers?"
- "How do we distribute multimedia content over the Net without worrying about users having the right helper applications?"
- "How do we create multiuser environments where people can share documents and collaborate in real time without a steep learning curve?"
- "How do you provide a package of protocols and services so our technically unsophisticated audience can utilize advanced services?"
- "How do we build computer-based training and online help into the applications?"

- "How do we easily and efficiently update content and upgrade the software people use to get at it, assuring that everyone is using the latest version?"

- "How do we make our sites more navigable and integrate vast databases?"

And it seemed like they were all asking me. It's good I had an answer.

Java.

II. Fluent Java

"When you help the shepherd,

you're helping the sheep."

—Jim Bakker explaining object-oriented programming to Jessica Hahn in a Florida hotel room

## CHAPTER 6

Java: The Man, The Legend

Many claims are being made about Java. Some hail it as the Cyber-Messiah. Some revile it as a Satan in sheep's clothing. Public relations departments on both sides of the fence are getting the word out:

What it can do, what it means for our economy, how it affects business systems, how it will transform digital communications, how it will mend the tears in the time-space continuum, how it will cure cancer!

When Java was introduced, the first task of its promoters was to educate programmers who were developing in C and C++. For it to become universally accepted, the education process had to be extended to network managers, system administrators, multimedia designers and producers, corporate executives, and ultimately the general public, who might eventually need to be swayed to buy an inexpensive Java-capable device for most computing chores rather than a full-blown personal computer.

While it will ultimately achieve mass-market consumer brand-recognition status, the fact that Java is a programming language cannot be ignored. Programming languages are not accustomed to being cultural icons. How many people know that their favorite multimedia CD-ROM was scripted in Lingo? Or that the word processor they depend on was built in C? So, for those of you who came to Java from the real world, rather than the sheltered world of people who understand their computers better than their kin, we will take your interest in Java as an opportunity to learn a bit about how programmers make computers and humans work together.

Java vs. The Boyscouts of America

or, How Java Helps an Old Lady Across the Information Superhighway.

TABLE 1.

Boy scouts	Java
Trustworthy	Simple
Loyal	Object oriented
Helpful	High performance
Friendly	Robust
Courteous	Secure
Kind	Portable
Obedient	Interpreted
Cheerful	Compiled
Thrifty	Multithreaded
Brave	Dynamic
Clean	Distributed
Reverent	Architecture neutral

Java: The Language

Java is a language. Languages can convey many things. They can produce beautiful poetry and insane ramblings as well as soothing hymns and pompous orations. Before we get into the grammar, syntax and spelling, we should know more about the culture, the region, the nature of Java.

Is Java guttural? Arcane? Lilting? Martial? Brogue? Compelling? Seductive? Cloying? Mellifluous? Loud?

To understand this language, we need to put it in context. We need to study the animal that utters Java and the animal that listens. The animal that transports Java and the animal that receives it. We must study:

Where it lives (its habitat), how it responds to stimuli (behavior), what it looks like (markings), what it consumes, what it excretes, how it disposes of its waste, how it mates, how it takes care of its young.

Let's look at Java in its natural habitat: the network. And what better network to study than the Global Internet, a nesting area for a diverse range of Java programs. Looking at its use on the Internet, we can apply what we've learned to the corporate intranet, which is nothing more than the application of successful Internet technologies in a more controlled environment.

Java: The Webmaster's Friend

Whether on the Internet or intranet, the Webmaster's job is not an easy one. Users want their Webs to do more and more, interface with databases, archive discussions, capture user information, promote products and balance the checkbook. And the tools just haven't been available. Almost all "interactivity" is provided through forms on the user end and PERL scripts or C code running in the Common Gateway Interface (CGI) between HTTPD (the HyperText Transfer Protocol Daemon, or Webserver) and other software packages running on the server, such as a context-based search engine that has indexed the HTML files, a relational database or a system that tracks your preferences by sending back to the client identifying information with each page or requesting the user's identity new input needs to be added to a profile (such as a shopping cart application). Because the Web browser can speak only to the Web server and not directly with the other applications, there is always some performance loss in the content handling. Because the input from the Web browser and the output to the browser must be formatted in HTML to be displayed, content that is natively stored in other forms (such as in a database server) must often be massaged twice: as input and as output.

Even on a high-capacity, low-latency network, interactivity is stymied by the basic architecture. The user has to read instructions, fill out forms, submit them for processing and wait for a reply from the server before moving on. There is no feedback from the Web until the cycle is completed.

## CHAPTER 7

Imagemap: Server-side (CGI) to Client-side (Java)

Besides adding attractive graphics, there haven't been many ways to distinguish pages. One of the few tricks available to the Webmaster to create a real GUI (Graphical User Interface) is the imagemap. To create an imagemap, the Webmaster uses a program that defines regions, by pixels, on the graphic and creates a file that will be moved to the server. When a region of the imagemap is clicked (the client and server know it's an imagemap because of the ISMAP tag where the graphic is displayed), the browser sends a notice to the imagemap program in the cgi-bin (CGI binaries) to look at the map file and deliver the appropriate document referenced by the region of the graphic selected by the mouse click.

In a server side imagemap, there are four necessary elements:

`http://www.lab.com/LiveJava/developer/ImageMap.html`

1. An HTML File to hold the imagemap graphic.
2. Imagemap software in CGI-bin on the server with the correct MIME-types set.

For example, this is the one on the Netsite server:

```
type=magnus-internal/imagemap   exts=map
```

The map file will not returned as a text document. Instead, the imagemap operation is performed and the correct document returned to the user..

3. The graphic.

4. The map file on the server.

```
#
#----------------> Live Java ImageMap file <-------------

#
#----------------> H O M E   P A G E <---------------
#
#    map file: /opt/home/www/pub/imaps/LiveJava.map
#    gif file: /opt/home/www/pub/husky/lab/LiveJava.gif
#
#    For now, Default is home page
default http://www.lab.com/LiveJava/
#
#
#The Juke Box links to the database section
rect   http://www.lab.com/LiveJava/developer/dbase.html   75,23
328,70
#
#
#    Paymaster links to business section
circ http://www.lab.com/LiveJava/developer/business.html 15,85
103,170
#
#    For the actual imagemap file, look at the above URL
```

Instant replay of the CGI-based Imagemap:

The HTML file that presented the server-side imagemap included nothing more than a reference to the graphic that is displayed, the location of the map file on the server that links the coordinates with the locations, and a note to the server that the graphic is a map <ISMAP> so that the imagemap software on the server will be called.

1. Everything is on server. Client browses to a location with an imagemap.
2. Server sends html page and graphic to browser.
3. Browser holds graphic/HTML ISMAP tag. Server holds imagemap software/mapfile
4. User clicks on imagemap, sends commands to server that determines what document to send next.

There are several problems with this system. The user has no more information on what will happen when the mouse is clicked then what is provided on the graphic. There is no elegant way to annotate the imagemap, provide online guidance as to what the user will find behind the map region, or to let the user jump to a particular subdirectory. Generally, this has made the imagemap more decorative than functional, with explanatory text below, that might provide jumps beyond the first-level directories to other information on the server.

Many people have asked of the Web: "why can't this work like any regular GUI, with pop-up menus as you move the mouse over buttons?" The problem has been that the Webmaster, content developer or Web producer has had control only over the server. Once the HTML page, with graphics and all, is on the user's desktop, it cannot respond to the user. The Webmaster can only set up server software that waits for more responses from the user's machine, as mousec licks on hyperlinks or the input from forms. What if the Webmaster's reach could be fully extended to the user's desktop?

How does the media producer provide new capabilities to the end user without having control over the application development? The Webmaster has been at the mercy of software developers, learning new extensions to HTML, new media file formats, new server configurations to take advantage of new capabilities, all the while deciding how to incorporate new capabilities into the site. This is a bit backward. How a Web site is designed and implemented should be driven by the user's needs, not what capabilities are built into the client and server software.

With each new capability, the Webmaster has had to come to terms with backward compatibility. How do you increase the capabilities while keeping the site functional for browsers with different formatting and different capabilities. Even HTML might not meet the Webmaster needs. The Webmaster might want to develop a different SGML DTD to handle a particular content type. The Java applet provides a way for the producer to distribute an executable application along with the text, graphics, audio and other media files. The end user then interacts with the applet on the user's desktop computer, receiving instantaneous feedback from keystrokes or movements of the mouse across the window.

An applet is a Java application designed to run within the context of a Web browser. It is downloaded with other file types, causing activity and advanced user-interface properties on the desktop. It waits for events caused by the user's responses and then generates more activity. It can call on other applets and documents to create a self-contained but distributed multimedia platform.

By bundling the executable applications with the media content, the Webmaster's reach has permeated cyberspace, for better or worse. There will certainly be abuses of this new power: hostile applets or just poorly designed ones that tie up a system without giving much back, or simply useless gizmos that make the user feel like a chump for waiting the extra time on download. For an applet to be elegantly integrated into a site, its function must arise from a particular need. Applets become another element that must be balanced according to good design practices.

Before we get too deep into Java and how it can be used, let's take a quick look at a popular use of Java on the Web, the interactive imagemap. While a server-side imagemap is static within the browser and simply references locations based on the area of the imagemap selected by the mouse click, a Java-based imagemap has areas that change as the mouse moves over them. What happens within the image is completely up to the Java programmer. Sounds can be played, characters brought to life, scrolls unfurled. This is because the applet is a program delivered from the server that runs on within the browser on the users computer, and immediately responds to events on the desktop.

When to use Java in an imagemap

A Webmaster often has to decide when to use an imagemap, and when to use separate icons. Generally, an imagemap is used when the information is most clearly presented as regions on one graphic. There are pros and cons to using imagemaps. When Penguin Books set up a Web site, they offered the choice between text-based and graphical interface. The text-based interface was more useful but did not capture the corporate identity. Like graphics, applets are not by nature good or bad. They can be useful or just annoying. Here are three examples of Java used in an imagemap.

Appropriate use:

When the mouse is moved over a topic heading on an imagemap, it shows subtopics on a scroll-down bar. The subtopics can be selected to skip the first-level index of subdirectories. The link that will respond to the mouse click is highlighted visually. Audio augments the text with additional information and does not simply repeat what is on the screen.

Inappropriate use:

When the mouse is moved over a part of the graphic, an announcer's voice recites the words that are clearly labeled or animates an icon for no particular reason.

Indeterminate use:

When the mouse is moved over an icon, completely random sounds occur. Icons shift to another icon that makes the user question what will actually happen when the mouse button is clicked.

Imagemap as an Applet

The issue of creating interactive imagemaps gives us the opportunity to understand what an applet is and how it works. We've explained the mechanics of the server-side imagemap and it's elements: the graphic, the CGI program and the map file. With the Java-based imagemap, no special software needs be running on the server, as the software is delivered to the client computer along with the graphics and text (and other media, such as audio).

We'll go into the nuts and bolts of setting up Java-based Web services in the next section. Here, we're just understanding the basic mechanics:

A Web page (HTML file) is requested by the browser. Like any HTML file, it contains references to other files that should be pulled in. In the server-side example, the HTML file brought along with it the graphic. In this case, it brings along with it an applet, or executable application.

Unlike the CGI-based imagemap, which included a reference to software running on the server, this javatized HTML file pulls the imagemap software itself from the server and executes it in the browser. As far as HTML/HTTP (the Web) is concerned, nothing but the executable application and some accompanying text is fetched from the server. No graphics, no audio, no text to be displayed by the browser. These are all part of the applet.

```
http://www.lab.com/LiveJava/developers/ImageMap.html

<HTML>
<HEAD>
<TITLE>Live Java ImageMap Javatized Version</TITLE>
</HEAD>
<body><center>
<applet codebase="applets/ImageMap"
        code=ImageMap.class
        width=522
        height=486>
<param name=img value="LiveJava.gif">
<param name=highlight value="brighter30">
<param name=area1 value="RoundHrefBut
  tonArea,15,85,103,170,sixty/
index.html">

<param name=area52 value="HrefBut
  tonArea,69,254,167,350,catalogs/index.htm">
<param name=area2
value="SoundArea,260,180,120,60,audio/hi.au">
<param name=area2 value="NameArea,260,180,120,60,Hi!">
<param name=area3 value="NameArea,265,125,45,20,That
  is my right eye">
<param name=area4 value="NameArea,335,130,45,20,That
  is my left eye">
<param name=area5 value="HrefButtonArea,200,7,210,300,/
~flar/">
<param name=area6 value="RoundHrefBut
  tonArea,15,85,103,170,sixty/index.html">
<param name=area10 value="AnimA
  rea,xx,xx,xx,xx,blah.html>
<param name=area7 value="SoundArea,425,98,27,27,audio/
chirp1.au">
<param name=area8 value="NameArea,425,98,27,27,Chirp!">
<param name=area9 value="ClickArea,0,0,522,486">
</applet>
</body></html>
```

Of all the extensions to HTML, the Applet DTD is probably the most significant. It informs the browser that an area is to be set aside for an executable application to run within the Web page. It tells the browser where to get this applet, how much space it will require and some parameters for this specific implementation of the applet. These parameters are predefined within the applet and tell the applet where to get the materials to do its work, such as graphics, audio, and other small programs it can run.

<applet codebase="applets/ImageMap"

The first line informs the Java-enabled browser where to get the software it's going to run. If the codebase is not specified, it assumes by default that all reference to code is relative to the base URL of the document, or document base, where the HTML file was stored. The codebase can be set relative to the document base, or it can be a URL specifying any location on the Internet.

code=ImageMap.class

This tells the browser what bytecodes to download. This .class file is the essence of the applet, the executable application that the browser interprets and runs. The .class file is created when the Java source code is compiled, or changed from a human-readable text file into a browser-readable format. This is very much like machine code that is read by computer hardware, but as we will see, this machine language is produced for an abstract, virtual machine that is not tied to any particular hardware platform. This virtual machine specification is made real by the Java-interpreter within the browser, which runs the bytecodes as a software program.

width=522
height=486>

This is the space defined on the Web page for the applet to run within. The applet can launch other windows and perform outside this frame, but some space must be reserved for the applet.

```
<param name=img value="penguinmast.gif">
<param name=highlight value="brighter30">
```

```
<param name=area1 value="RoundHrefBut
  tonArea,15,85,103,170,sixty/
index.html">
```

The parameters that the applet will recognize are specified in the Java source code, which are then present in the .class file or bytecodes. The parameters have two attributes, name, which is referenced in the applet. At a certain point while the applet is running, it will look for a particular parameter. When it finds it by name, it will look at the value of the parameter it is reading so that it can take some sort of action, such as displaying a particular image. For example, when it comes time to display an image, the applet will look for the name of a parameter called img and then the particular image specified by the value will be imported.

This is what a relevant line of Java source code might look like within an imagemap applet:

```
baseImage = getImage(getDocumentBase(),
getParameter("img"));
```

## CHAPTER 8

The Java Dialectic:
Interpreted and Compiled

At the heart of Java's capabilities is a basic dichotomy, that Java is both a compiled and an interpreted language. After source code is written, it's compiled into bytecodes. These are then interpreted at run time on the client machine. The compiler is written according to a virtual machine specification, which makes Java code highly, and immediately, portable and architecture neutral. Its security features, which will be discussed later, are built on the fact that the run-time interpretation also checks for anomalies in the code that could result from a programmer tampering with the compiler to defeat safety restrictions on applet behavior. The run-time buffer and preloading of bundles of code (called classes and packages) allow the applets themselves to be small, simple and compact.

Java is Interpreted

Some other languages that are interpreted: SmallTalk, TCL, and PERL.

I put this first, because it provides a framework for understanding many of the other features of the Java language, such as its portability and openness (architecture neutrality), as well as its robustness, simplicity and ease of development, prototyping and fast, fearless implementation.

Because it is interpreted, the code is written to be run within a familiar environment, no matter what the underlying hardware or operating system. PERL has become the de facto standard for server-side CGI programming as PERL scripts are relatively easy to write and the PERL interpreter is available on most platforms. This makes it highly portable, as calls are not made to the underlying computer or operating system, but only to the PERL executable program. A Java programmer, like a PERL programmer, has an exact specification for what will happen during the run-time of the code, as the loop is closed. The commands the programmer writes are exact matches to functions understood by the executable binary file that runs on particular computer platform. This is a key to Java's simplicity.

One reason that PERL has been so successful on the Web is that there is a default interface: the Web browser, with its ability to input data through forms. CGI programs operate faster in C, but with all the latencies associated with the Web, the slow performance is rarely noticeable. PERL has no windowing environment or interface toolkit, but it acts very well as a content handler for input from messages coming from a nice presentation layer, such as the browser provides. OraPERL is an example of a fairly robust library of scripts that work as a communications layer between the Oracle Relational Database on the back end, the Web server in the middle, and the browser on the front-end. Between them, the developer has much of the power of Oracle with an expensive proprietary, rapid development interface. Many shopping cart systems on the Web are written in PERL, as well as BBSs (bulletin board systems), as it does a good job taking information, massaging it, and presenting it to another program or in a terminal window. The major drawback is lack of control over the interface, beyond the capabilities of HTML.

TCL (Tool Command Language) is another simple, interpreted scripting language used to develop Web sites and stand-alone applications.

It distinguishes itself from PERL by having a GUI interface toolkit, Tk. Tcl is used to create small applications very quickly and tie together existing applications. its syntax is simple and structure is not generally relevant.

Tcl/Tk was developed at Sun Labs and for a while, before the advent of Java, promised to become the predominant scripting platform for Internet development. Some Tcl/Tk developers were upset when Java was introduced to the Internet, as it seemed that Sun had produced a competitor for its own product. Java, though, is more complex and structured, which makes it more difficult to do really simple things. It looked like the Tcl and Java would make a good team, until Sun and Netscape teamed up to create Javascript, which is very much like Tcl. In fact, it's a lot like Java except that it's not compiled.

Java is Compiled

Some Languages that are compiled: C, C++

What makes Java so original is the fact that it's both interpreted and compiled. Rather than interpreting a human-readable scripting language, the run-time interpreter receives efficient bytecodes generated by a compiler. These bytecodes are very similar to native machine instructions, missing only the pieces that know about the idiosyncrasies of the hardware platform or operating system, which the interpreter knows about, having been developed independently and optimized for a particular computer platform. The production-time compiling dramatically improves the performance of Java over pure scripting languages.

When the Java source code is first compiled into bytecodes, a class file is created. This class file is a set of tokens representing actions that the computer running the Java program will take. If real-time capabilities, meaning guaranteed, timed performance, are required of a Java application, these tokens can be dynamically translated into native machine code through more advanced garbage-collection methods than are available in first-generation compilers and interpreters.

Compilers are used to cut development time and aid portability, but at the expense of raw application speed. While hand-tooled assembly code is still the way to produce applications that take full advantage of all the operations of the particular computer, the drawback is the application is locked into one environment. This is great for the internal development teams for business systems in a large corporation, which typically has a primary, centralized computer architecture. Assembly languages are not so good for software developers who need to distribute their code to users on diverse platforms, and internal business system developers now facing increasingly heterogeneous client-server environments. The compiler knows a lot about the file and directory structure of the operating system and the features of the hardware platform and makes from the source code an executable binary. The source application can be ported to another platform by modifying the source code to account for the major differences, then recompiling in the new environment. Java's combination of being precompiled into bytecodes and then running on a virtual machine environment that is representation, in software, of a silicon computer and optimized for the host computer's architecture creates a high-performance operating environment while maintaining the portability and ease of development of a fully interpreted language.

## CHAPTER 9

Java Language Basics

The Phenomenology of Java

Spinoza wrote that everything is one substance and that thought and extension are two attributes of the same substance. In the Spinozistic universe, any object is a mode of this substance and is defined by its thought and extension. This was revolutionary in the Cartesian world, where Mind and Body were considered an unassailable dichotomy. Spinoza said that the Mind is the idea of the Body, and the Body an extension of the Mind. Descartes said I think therefore I am. Descartes would have been an imperative programmer. Procedural. Based on statements. Not object oriented.

Although he might have been an imperative programmer in a later age, Descartes was an analytic philosopher, breaking problems down to their foundation in order to solve them, which of course only led to a new set of questions to answer. He set out to prove the existence of God mathematically. Logically. Geometrically. Spinoza, on the other hand, started with definitions, such as a definition of God. He started out with several modular solutions. Axioms. Propositions. And from there he built an understanding of Humanity. In object-oriented programming, you don't have to break anything down. You just use the objects as extensions to presolved problems.

All object-oriented programming does is encapsulate the instance variables (attributes, data, state) and the methods (functions, behaviors) in one place. It is tempting to think of objects as Leibniz's monads, but they are very different. Monads do not have methods that allow them to communicate with other monads. They are, as Leibniz said, windowless. Monads are driven by preset rules. They are basically just attributes that all act independently of one another, like the bulbs in a Las Vegas marquee that appear to be swirling downward toward the entrance to a nightclub but are in fact only blinking on and off according to their internal timing. Objects affect one another. It is unclear whether Leibniz was convinced of his theory of monadology or was trying to account for predestination and an omnipotent creator, who simply set his creation in motion according to his clockwork plan. Whatever his thinking, he created a world of attributes with no real behavior, just the appearance of behavior.

This is how many people view computers and computer programs. Once upon a time, computers were just calculators that performed functions according to preset internal rules and according to the data that the user entered into the computer at the console, off punchcards, magnetic tape, disk drives, or over networks. Computers, unless buggy, should be predictable machines. Now computers are used to perform ever more complicated communications and modeling tasks over ever more heterogeneous networks. The experience of using a computer is becoming more organic and unpredictable. Java was created not only to compute but to live and to thrive. We realize that software is not something written by a human and then distributed and used, but is inhabited by humans and constantly evolving. Rather than Leibniz's monadology, the modern network is becoming Deleuze's nomadology.

## CHAPTER 10

Attributes and Behaviors

An object is a software model of an idea or a thing. In other words, a model of a real thing or a model of a concept. The two important features of a real object, a concept or a software model are its *attributes* and its *behavior.* Think of a billiard ball. Its attributes are its mass, its color, and its position on the table in relation to the other balls and the cushions. Attributes can also describe the object's state: whether it is in motion or still.

As an attribute determines what an object *is,* an object's behavior determines what an object *does* in response to changes in its internal state or through the influence of other objects. Taking its attributes and its behaviors together, a billiard ball has momentum and inertia. It has the ability to affect and influence other objects and be affected in turn by their *attributes and behavior.* The cue ball will behave in a generally determined way when affected by the cue stick; the stripes and solids will exhibit their behavior when acted upon by the cue ball.

Instance Variables. The cue ball has different attributes than the other balls (stripes and solids). It has more heft. It is white. If the cue ball were a Java object, these features of its state would be its *instance variables*, or the particular variables that define the attributes of the object. These are internal to the ball. Unshared. Each ball has its own *instance variables* just as it has its own attributes or properties that make it what it is. Think of this as the core, or inner being of the object. The thing in itself. The soul of the object. *Instance variables* define the object's attributes and state.

Say our object was the eight ball. Instance variables might include:

```
Ball.Striped = False
Ball.Color = Black
```

Instance variables for all balls would include:

Xposition, Yposition, Xvelocity, Yvelocity, XAcceleration, YAcceleration, Mass, Elasticity.

If you don't set your instance variables right, say, elasticity set to 0 and mass way too high, the eight ball might shatter on impact instead of being sent to the corner. If elasticity is high and hardness low, like a piece of cookie dough, it might just get dented and sit there. The instance variables themselves cannot be changed by any outside objects. So how does the state of the object change? How does it get dented? It's fine to know whether it's moving or still but something else to set it in motion.

Methods. As an object's attributes and state are defined by its instance variables, its behavior is defined by its *methods*. Methods define how an object can be effected, how it interfaces with the other objects in the world, and how it can change its own state.

Our eight ball has speed and acceleration variables of 0 as it sits on the table. The only method it needs is a "struck" method. When the "struck" method is invoked:

Ball.Struck (xforce, yforce)

enough information should be passed from one object to another to allow each to change its state information (direction, acceleration, etc.) In Java and other OO jargon this is known as *messaging.* The cushion and the wooden cue have different elasticities than a ball. Balls move at different angles and with varying degrees of force. But each object is aware of its own attributes and state, and when the struck method is invoked, will pass along all the information required to allow the struck object to alter its state, sending it in a new direction at a new speed. Again, each object knows its own state information (attributes): elasticity/hardness, force, direction and can invoke the struck method. Each ball knows of nothing else.

Actually, programming a complete billiards game in Java is significantly less complex than programming the game in an imperative or procedural language, when so many more factors need to be accounted for on a bird's-eye level, from the perspective of the user or of the game as a whole. Building a robust, evocative game is even easier as we begin to understand OO concepts such as class inheritance and ones in which Java is particularly featureful, such as the major packages, GUI toolkit and threads. Once the basic game is built, factors such as wind, increased gravity, or rubber cues can be added. A friction property (attribute) can be added to the table that would allow the players to experiment with pool on a surface of ice, sand, or chewing gum. It is fairly easy to understand how these new *instance variables* and *methods* would alter the game.

CHAPTER 11   *Classes, Subclasses, and Inheritance*

In the real world, God doesn't have to create everything individually every day. In the beginning were a few good concepts; things haven't varied substantially since. Most of the objects in the world today have descended from previous objects. Actually, all of them have. And they all inherit some characteristics, whether animal, vegetable or mineral. A dressmaker doesn't have to make every piece of clothing from scratch, a conceptual blank slate; a "clean-room implementation" of the mini-skirt never would have happened, as if a dress had never been made before. Fashion evolves. To write a fugue, a composer interweaves motifs, variations on a theme. In our billiards game, we don't have to create every individual object from original clay. In other words, a programmer doesn't have to reinvent the wheel every time he needs a new wheel. Whether its a mag wheel for a 'vette, or a training wheel for a bike, any particular wheel will inherit some properties from the class of wheels, or it just wouldn't be a wheel.

Many different objects can be *instantiated* from one single class, much as many dresses can be derived from a pattern, each with a different fabric and design. As Plato would have it, any particular leaf is an implementation of the leafy ideal. Nietzsche would argue that the concept of the ideal Leaf is a mistake of language. Because we have a word "leaf" we have conceptualized Leaf, rather than accepting leaves. Java code is somewhere in between. Objects are continually being instantiated from classes in a way that suits a particular need. As is conventional in philosophy where the Ideal is capitalized and the real is in lower case, in Java the Class is generally capitalized and the object is in lower case.

When two players step up to the pool table to begin a game (by hitting the Web page with their browsers, for example, and dropping an e-quarter into the slot), a rack appears with 15 balls in a triangular configuration with a slightly larger white ball a little way away. Rather than program each ball with its own characteristics, the OO developer would first create a Ball class that would have the basic attributes and methods of a billiard ball. The programmer does this by writing text in a file called Ball.java. Later, the programmer compiles the Ball source file into a Ball.class, as we will do shortly. The Ball class might have a radius, color, position, velocity, and other state information, such as whether or not it's moving. When the Ball is first declared, its state information might look something like this:

```
class Ball
```

When it comes time to actually use a ball, you would code:

```
Ball poolball
```

This would instantiate a poolball object derived from the Ball class. Because objects are reusable, you could as easily derive a soccerball from the Ball class:

```
Ball soccerball
```

This is the a major benefit of object-oriented programming. Once the Ball class is defined, any new type of ball can be derived from that class. For example, a cue ball, a stripe or a solid would inherit properties (attributes and methods) from the Ball class. An individual ball, say the nine ball, would be derived from, or inherit properties from, the subclass stripe.

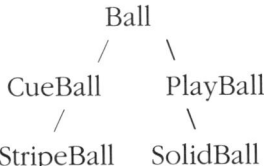

When you were ready to code EightBall.java to create a new class that had some new attributes and behaviors, such as starting out at the center of the rack, being black, and causing the game to end when it is sunk, you could start by importing Ball, which will allow you to refer to the Ball class, then state that

```
class EightBall extends Ball
```

which means that it has access to (inherits) Ball's attributes and behaviors and will extend them to do something new.

Whether you create a separate class to handle the eight ball or just create an instance of the SolidBall class when the game starts:

```
PoolBall eight = new PoolBall("solid", "black", "8")
```

When an event occurs, the Ball (**if this.numeral = 8)** can perform differently than if that state information reports that the ball is not an EightBall.

A cue ball and a solid or stripe on the table (balls 1 through 15) are objects that inherit properties (attributes and behaviors, state information and methods) from a common class (Ball). An object is an instance of a class. It would persist for the duration of a game, as a usable and malleable instance of a class. A subtle but not insignificant feature of object-oriented programming is that the object can outlive the object that created it. It can be passed to another object across a network to perform in a different capacity.

Classes are not objects, but templates or blueprints that define how an object will appear and perform when the object is created. An object is an *instance* of a class. It is *instantiated,* or comes into being, when the program is run. The core, or nucleus, or soul of the object is its *instance variables,* or the data that is packaged or encapsulated within the object. That soul is wrapped in *methods* that provide its interface to other objects and the world at large. All communication between souls is mediated by methods. If an object is to affect another object, its methods will interact with the methods of the second object, which will alter that object's instance variables.

This leads us to another notion. If StripeBall is a subclass of Ball (StripeBall extends Ball), it would be make sense that a general class of strikable objects might help us construct the cushions, cues, pockets and table. We could call it the Equipment class.

```
import Equipment;

public class Pocket
        extends Entity_Implementation_Base
        implements Equipment, StrikableObject {
```

The same thing would be found at the beginning of the Ball source code.

```
import Equipment;

public class Ball
        extends Equipment
        implements Equipment, StrikableObject {

public Ball() {

        position = new Point();
        velocity = new Vector();
        stationary = true;
        ballColor = Color.white;
    }
```

If we revisit the family tree, we might see

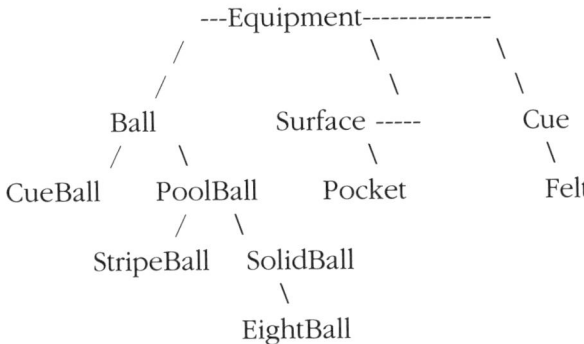

```
              ---Equipment-------------
             /               \          \
            /                 \          \
         Ball              Surface -----    Cue
        /    \                  \            \
  CueBall   PoolBall        Pocket         Felt
           /    \
   StripeBall   SolidBall
                   \
               EightBall
```

CHAPTER 12   *The Java Class Libraries*

An obvious question arises. Object -oriented programming is easy if you already have some code to work with. You have a Ball.class, which is a great model of a ball, so can start to model other balls and instantiate them as objects in programs. The balls are derived from the Equipment.class. So where do you start? At the library.

Just as there are some common elements in our language that allow humans to communicate (some argue the foundation of this is the structure of the sentence, some argue it is the archetypal symbolic elements), the Java programmer is assured that a certain body of knowledge will await the applet at the execution end of its journey across the network. These classes, the Java Class Libraries, provide the basic functionality for writing Java programs. For the complete Java API, see the documentation on **www.javasoft.com** (a.k.a. **java.sun.com**). Commercial Java development environments, such as Symantec *Cafe* for Windows95 and NT, *Roaster* for the Macintosh and *Java Workshop (JDE)* for Solaris, provide a bird's-eye view of the Java packages and allow you to select a package for import with a point-and-click interface. Here are the six class libraries that are included in any commercial implementation of the Java interpreter. They are also known as Packages. You can create your own packages of classes to organize your code and make programming and distribution of classes more efficient.

Interfaces and Inheritance

Just as classes are abstract templates for objects that will be instantiated, an interface is a placeholder for a collection of related methods that can be made available to your class. An interface declares that an object will have a certain set of methods, regardless of its parent.

In Java, a class can have only one progenitor, from which it inherits its characteristics. This would mean, were it not for *interfaces*, that it would have access only to the variables and methods of its parents. Other object-oriented languages solve this with "multiple inheritance," allowing a class to extend more than one other class. To keep Java simple and allow classes to share in common methods, a class can implement an interface, an abstract method belonging to a package. Because they are not classes or objects, but abstract methods, interfaces are not instantiated, they are implemented to run them within the program.

The Java Language Foundation Package

java.lang

This package contains the core classes and interfaces that make up the Java language API. Java language package features include strings, objects, and math functions. Some of the classes within the java.lang package provide keys to programming in Java, others are simply "wrapper classes," which provide a means of treating very basic data structures (called types, such as **char, int, float**) as objects (**Character, Integer, Float**).

Interfaces

Runnable

Methods that can be used for running classes as independent threads without having to inherit the Thread class, which is not always possible as Java supports only single inheritance (a class can extend only one other class and thereby inherits the properties of its parents, grand parents, great-grandparents and on up). This is a little piece of the Thread class, an abstract method, that can be accessed by any class no matter what package it belongs to.

Classes

Object

The most basic class, analogous to $root_class (#1) in MOO. All other classes are derived from this.

Thread

Defines an independent means of execution, a key concept in Java's multithreaded nature. Any object or bit of code can be assigned to its own thread, so multiple parts of the Java applet/application can be run simultaneously. Related to the Runnable interface. Any object that implements the Runnable interface is expected to run as an independent thread.

String

A string is a sequence of characters, such as "hello." All strings in Java are derived from the String class. There is no built-in "string" type, as there are for ints and floats.

| Exception | Exceptions are part of what makes Java so robust. When a program can't find a resource it needs, it doesn't just crash but throws exceptions, and a piece of code must watch for that exception so that it can handle the "error" gracefully without crashing the program. So instead of GPFs (General Protection Faults) we have NullPointerExceptions. |

Wrapper Classes

| Character | A character is one keyboard stroke, such as "a." Characters include meta-characters, such as \n for the enter key and \t for tab. You can have an array of characters, such as {"a", "b", "c"}. This is not the same as a string, such as "abc." **char** is a built-in type. The Character class is used when a **char** needs to be treated like an object. |

| Integer | An integer is a positive or negative whole number. No decimals. All integers in Java contain 32 bits. This range gives you about -2 billion to +2 billion. Integer (or int) can represent between -2147483648 and 2147483647. |

| Float | For "real number" values that contain decimals. The maximum value a float can have is 3.40282346638528860e+38. The minimum value a float can have is 1.40129846432481707e-45. |

| Long | A "long" is a 64-bit integer, for dealing with very small or very large whole numbers. |

| Double | A float with greater precision (more decimal places). The maximum value a double can |

have is 1.79769313486231570e+308d. The minimum value a double can have is 4.94065645841246544e-324d.

The Java Utilities Package

java.util

Computational aids such as date conversion, vectors, random number generators.

Interfaces

Enumeration | Important for the Vector class. The enumeration interface defines that an object contains some collection of things. Your object can determine if you are at the end of a series or to get the next element from the series.

Classes

Date | A way to get the local machine's date or for working with and comparing dates and times.

Random | A (pseudo) random number generator. Can produce a random integer, long, float, double, or 'gaussian' value.

Vector | Similar to an array, a vector encapsulates a collection of objects. Objects can be added to or removed from the vector, and the vector will grow dynamically as new objects are added. Unlike an array, which has a fixed length determined upon creation.

StringTokenizer   Parses a string into a series of tokens based on a specified delimeter set. For example, "hello, how are you" can be broken into the tokens "hello", "how", "are", "you" based on the delimiter " ", (space"). We've made much use of the String Tokenizer for parsing Moon-Bean protocol messages, but most people will not.

Java Input/Output Classes

java.io

Flows information into and out of windows, ports, and sockets and between applets.

Interfaces

DataInput   Your object will act as a DataInputStream, and your object will define the readInt() methods.

DataOutput   Your object will act as a DataOutputStream and will define the writeInt() methods.

Classes

InputStream   A Stream at its highest abstraction defines a flow of data and does not concern itself with the representation of the data. It can be binary data moving over a socket, or text data from a file, or keyboard input, etc. An InputStream will allow you to read from this data stream.

OutputStream	This will allow you to write to the data stream. An object that needs to read and write, such as a Socket, will contain both InputStreams and OutputStreams. Printers or displays would need only an OutputStream for writing.
DataInputStream	From the DataInputStream, objects can read precise bits of data, with its readByte(), read-Char(), readInt(), and readLine() methods.
DataOutputStream	For writing with writeInt(), writeChar(), Print-Stream() for writing whole lines of text with println(), as you would to a printer, socket or display.

Abstract Window Toolkit

java.awt

A very important package that contains all the classes for the Graphical User Interface components for constructing the layout. This allows the user to make selections, type input, read output, and otherwise use the mouse in relation to the content.

Classes

Frame	A titled window.
Event	Enables response to stimuli caused by the system or user input.
FontMetrics	Contains information about the shape, size and curves of characters.

Window	The basic unit of the graphic interface object.
MediaTracker	Monitors binary objects, such as graphics and audio, loaded over the network.
Dialog	Prompts for user input.
CheckBoxes	A selectable item.
TextFields	A fixed-size region of editable text.
TextArea	A multiline editable text field that can be scrolled.
Button	A push-button.
Label	A text label.
Graphics	For creating line art and painted areas.
Scrollbar	A scrollbar.
List	A scrolling list.

Java Network Classes

java.net

Provides network access capabilities based on Internet protocols.

Classes

URL	Defines a Uniform Resource Location, which can be broken into its individual components with the getProtocol() method ("http"), getH-

	ost() ("www.lab.com"), getPort() (80), and getFile() ("index.html").
InetAddress	Represents an Internet address in IP or alpha/domain form.
Socket	A connection to an Internet address and port. Socket contains an InputStream and Output-Stream for reading from and writing to the socket.
URLConnection	A connection to a URL that is more compli-cated than a socket. This could be used for writing to a Web browser, where a detailed understanding of the type of data coming through the stream is necessary. A URLCon-nection would be useful for transferring data by MIME-types, rather than something inter-active like Telnet.

Java Applet Classes

java.applet

Applet defines an object that can be embedded in a Web page, as opposed to a Java application which is not derived from Applet. An applet is delivered using HTTP from the Web server to the browser over the Web and is immediately executable in the browser.

Interfaces

AppletContext	An applet's context enables the applet to show a Web document or load an image in the Web browser or GUI element, such as displaying in a java.awt.Canvas object.

AudioClip	Defines the interface for an audio clip object with play(), stop() and loop() methods.

Classes

Applet	It is the superclass of all browser-embeddable Java applets.

## CHAPTER 13

Good Things in Small Packages

The packages listed above are bundles of related classes that are provided as part of the Java development and run-time environments. To use these in a Java application or applet, you would create, or declare, a class that extends (inherits the properties of) a class that's part of the Java Class Libraries. Most likely, any applet you load off the Internet will use a combination of custom-coded classes delivered off the server and packages of classes that will already be located on your client computer and are guaranteed to be present on all Java-enabled systems. A third type of package that can be utilized by applet developers is custom, third-party packages that are preloaded on the client system. These are distributed in advance by disk, CD-ROM or file transfer over the Internet.

The developer of the package has tools to allow future and contemporary programmers to build on his work, without giving away his source code or allowing his work to be adversely affected. Such tools include *access controls*, which specify whether the classes within a package can be reused by the general public or are to remain unique to the package, and *javadoc,* which creates custom API documentation. The writer of new classes also has a tool, the *import statement*, that makes it easy to build on the work of the original Java designers and the creators of custom packages without calling every method and variable of every class by its full name. Another feature of Java attempts to guarantee that a class can be referenced across the Internet without naming conflicts. The naming conventions proposed as an Internet standard by the Java designers parallel domain name space. Just as a particular e-mail address (username@host.domain.name) is unique, a Java class, package, or method should be unique.

The Package Statement

Every class is part of a *package*. The first line of code in a Java source file states the name of the package to which the code belongs. If the package name is not stated, the class is part of a default package that includes the other classes stored in the same directory of the host computer. Java programs have access to all the classes in the package and by default (unless stated otherwise) all the methods and variables in those classes. In this way, a Java program is part of a family and easily inherits characteristics from its relatives. Not only does this limit the need to rewrite programs to use them in new ways and build on them easily, it also allows these programs to be called by familiar names rather than the long formal names.

For example, on MoonBean, the package statement looks like this:

```
package husky.mb;
```

Global Naming Convention

If we were to follow the naming convention developed by the Java designers to guarantee that nobody else uses the same package name, we wouldn't call it husky.mb, as someone at Husky Oil might write a program called MultiBurn and call their package husky.mb. As Java becomes more common on the Internet and people who publish their APIs and applets are dynamically referencing one another, uniqueness will be required, as two class files of the same name cannot occupy the same directory on a single host, and as we will see, package name by convention is tied to directory structure.

Because we are the only company in the world with the domain name LAB.COM, we are instructed to begin our package with our reverse name: COM.lab. Then, among users of this network, who happen to be employees of HuskyLabs, we might divide packages between ones we develop for our use and those of our customers and then put on the part of the package name that distinguishes it from other packages developed for our own use. This is the fully-qualified package name:

`COM.lab.husky.mb`

A class within the package, such as MBParser, would eventually become a foundation for new, more fully featured data-stream parsers. When this is needed, the new class might extend this fully qualified class name:

`COM.lab.husky.mb.MBParser`

If we are to write a new class outside this package that needs to invoke a method developed as part of the MoonBean package, such as doBrowse(), which pushes the MoonBean user to a new page, we would have to reference the fully qualified method name:

`COM.lab.husky.mb.MBParser.doBrowse()`

doBrowse(), which is internal to the MoonBean package, calls show-Document(), which is in the Java API (from the Java Class Libraries). showDocument() is a method that is part of the Applet package and implements AppletContext(), an Interface of java.applet. The fully qualified method that would need to be called is java.applet.Applet.AppletContext().showDocument(). It would get a bit cumbersome to reference complete package, class and method names constantly. The *import* statement provides a shortcut.

The Import Statement

Java classes are always available by their full name, if the classes can be read by the compiler and run by the interpreter. Importing packages and classes up front will allow you to refer to them by an abbreviated name throughout your code. The classes or packages are not actually imported with the statement but just make up a fully qualified name when a class or interface is being called in the file. If you plan to use several classes within a package, you can import them all with

```
import package.*
```

such as:

```
import java.net.*
import java.applet.*
import husky.mb.*
```

In theory, you should only import those classes you will be using so that the compiler can warn you if you try to use a class without implicitly importing it. You can specify the classes to import with:

```
import package.class
```

such as

```
import java.net.Socket
import java.net.URL
import java.applet.Applet
import husky.mb.MBparser
```

Access Controls

As we've discovered, objects are instances of classes. Objects are encapsulations of instance variables and methods. Methods in other classes, if they are aware of these variables and methods, can call these methods, build on them and alter them, unless they are protected from view. This is the core of Java's Object technology: once someone has invented a wheel, all you need to do is repaint it, and change the elasticity, durability, size, traction. The inventor of the wheel, however, needs to decide how much to share and with whom. That inventor has four options for control over the classes, methods, and variables and can declare the level of access individually on any method or variable or class.

Package

By default, if no protection is declared, the classes, variables and methods are available only to other classes within the same package. For example, MBWindow is a class in the MoonBean package that is a graphic interface, socket and stream all rolled into one. It is a window outside the browser, containing a menu bar, a place for the user to type, and an are for incoming text to be displayed. It also contains the cocket and its input/output streams. The MoonBean applet contains an instance of MBWindow (MBWindow window;) and MoonBean needs to be able to access the socket that's inside of its 'window' instance so it can initialize it, open it or close it. But this class should only be used by the MoonBean applet, not by other applets or classes that are not part of the MoonBean package, as they could wreak havoc on a MoonBean session. By default, if it is not declared public, private or protected, other classes within its package (the MoonBean package) will be able to access this object.

The MBWindow class declared with "package" (default) access controls:

```
class MBWindow extends Frame {
```

Instances of various classes (objects) are also left with default access controls:

```
WrappingTextArea display; //text output
Socket socket;            //telnet socket
PrintStream ostream;      //socket input stream
DataInputStream istream;  //socket output stream
Dialog loginDialog;       //username/pw box
TextField loginName;      //field for username
TextField loginPass;      //field for password
```

Public

While much of MBWindow used the default access controls, as it should be accessed only by MoonBean or other classes in the package, much of MoonBean itself needs to be called by the browser or appletviewer computer that will interpret and run the code. Declaring your classes, variables, and methods "public" will allow them to be viewed and used by any class anywhere. When you're getting started, it is often easiest to declare everything public, so that you don't start to "throw exceptions" (produce errors) when other classes need to access these methods; then you can limit access later.

First of all, the MoonBean class itself is declared public so it can be run in the browser, appletviewer or wherever its initiated on the network:

```
public class MoonBean extends Applet implements Runnable
{
```

Breaking this up grammatically, we have the *access control* declaration (**public**) the *class* (**MoonBean**), the *inheritance* (**java.applet.Applet**) and the *interface* (**Runnable**). Putting it back together, this means we have a new class that is an applet; at least, it inherits all the properties of the Applet class (and we know that it can refer to Applet by it's abbreviated name because **java.applet** must have been imported upfront). Because it inherits all of Applet's properties, it cannot inherit all the properties of another class. It needs to be run as an independent thread without extending the **java.lang.Thread**. So MoonBean implements the Runnable interface, which is part of the **java.lang** package, but is not a class and does not need to be inherited or instantiated.

Another example occurs farther down:

```
public static final String PRODUCTNAME = "MoonBean";
```

String productName creates a new instance of the **java.lang.String** class, called productName. "**=MoonBean**" preinitializes the product-Name object to that value, meaning that when the String class is instantiated, the productName object will be MoonBean. "**final**" makes the PRODUCTNAME String a constant that cannot be changed, even though it is public and hence visible. As in the programming language C, constants are capitalized throughout. "**static**" means the object is the same across all instances and belongs to the MoonBean class itself. And as we know, **public** means that it can be referenced (but not changed, since it's **final**) by any object. Why would you set this as public rather than the default package? No particular reason, except that other objects in other classes might one day need to get the productName. Perhaps to automatically display in a neon sign applet on other sites the fact that MoonBean is a featured product, among all the other products that need to be queried for their productName.

Protected and Private Protected

Subclasses are closely related to their parent classes and often need to alter the methods, variables, and data representations handed down to them. The *protected* level of access control allows a class and it's constituent parts to be visible to its progeny and other classes in the same package. *Private protected* access allows visibility to the classes' progeny, but not to other classes in the package.

Private

Methods and variables declared *private* are visible only to the class in which they are defined, not to any other class in the package, in its heritage or at large. Ideally, most of your code should be private, as classes need to know little about each other's internal representation to get the job done.

Storage

While the Java source code can have multiple classes defined within it, when the source is compiled, the classes will each occupy a separate .class file. In the source code, only one of the classes in a single .java file can be declared *public*. This class must have the same name as the source file (which will ultimately be the name as of .class file.)

On the system where the files are stored (locally or remotely), the directory structure must mirror the fully-qualified class name. For example, net.butterfly.husky.mb.MoonBean would be stored in com/lab/husky/mb/MoonBean.class (or if you are storing your files on a Windows system rather than UNIX, reverse the slashes.)

## CHAPTER 14

Finding the Right Class

Classpath

When it is time to compile EightBall.java into bytecodes as Eight-Ball.class, the compiler will need to find both of the other components of the package, such as SolidBall, from which it inherited many of its characteristics, and the components of the Java Class Libraries, from which many of its features are ultimately derived. On the end-user side, when the program is being interpreted and executed, the Java-enabled browser or desktop system must be able to find the classes that are being referenced. The *classpath* must be defined on your system for these classes to be found.

The Netscape browser is delivered with a file called moz2_X.zip (the X relating to the version number of Netscape being used). The file contains in a compressed format all the Java packages in the Java Class Libraries distribution. It must be referenced in your Classpath for Java applets to run when they are loaded by the browser over the network. Besides these basic libraries provided as part of the Java distribution, you might download to your local system and install classes provided by third- party developers or that you or someone in your organization might develop. These, too, need to be found at run time.

In UNIX, the directories where the classes might be found are separated by colons; under Windows, semicolons. In UNIX, the CLASSPATH variable is located in the .cshrc file if you're using the C shell, or the .profile if the Korn shell, or wherever your particular shell requires them. Under Windows, the classpath would be defined in the AUTOEXEC.BAT file.

A classpath under Windows with only the Java Development Kit installed might look like:

```
SET CLASSPATH=.;d:\java\lib\classes.zip
```

With Symantec *Cafe* (a Java development environment) and Netscape Navigator installed, the classpath might look like:

```
SETCLASS-
PATH=.;d:\Cafe\java\lib\classes.zip;D:\Wisock\Netscape\
Navigator\Program\java\classes
```

Here's an example classpath under UNIX:

```
setenv CLASSPATH /opt/home/motodave/.netscape:/usr/
local/java:/usr/local/java/bin:/usr/local/java/lib:/
usr/local/java:/usr/local/java/classes/husky:/usr/
local/java/classes:/usr/local/java/classes/mb::
```

As you can see, there are potentially required classes in several places on my computer. The classes for running MoonBean as a stand-alone Java application might be located in /usr/local/java/classes/mb, HuskyLabs custom database front-ends might be in /usr/local/java/classes/husky, and the Java Class Libraries are available in two places: /opt/home/motodave/.netscape (in the moz2_X.zip file for use by the Netscape browser) and /usr/local/lib (in classes.zip for use by the appletviewer and compiler included with the Java Development Kit).

In fact, you can actually compile Java source code using the class libraries included with Netscape browser, but it's easier to use dedicated tools for the job.

Under MacOS, there is no need to set the classpath, since the Mac is largely a single-user, single-state machine. File resources are always kept in places specific to the MacOS or the application. With Sun's JDK for the Mac, there is an option to set the classpath, but you don't need to if the Applet Viewer and the Compiler reside in the same folder as the Classes file. Sun's JDK also comes with a bunch of shared libraries that are placed in the Extensions folder of the System Folder. Netscape on the Mac doesn't use a classpath at all, as its classes are kept in files found in the Preferences folder of the System Folder.

CODEBASE

In the applet HTML tag, as discussed previously, the CODE and CODE-BASE are defined in the Web page. Now that we understand packages, how this is done will make more sense. The CODEBASE tag in the HTML page let's the browser know where to get the custom packages, stored in bytecodes, it will need run the Java program. This can be an Internet URL, where the code might be on a separate computer, or a relative path from the server root directory of public HTML files. If the applet's precompiled class file is in the same directory as the HTML file in which it is embedded, the CODEBASE tag is not necessary, as the class file will still be located. If the CODEBASE is specified, the CODE will be in a relative path to the codebase. Generally, classes are named according to directory structure, or stored according to naming conventions, depending on how you look at it. For example:

<applet   code="motodave/pool/billiards.class"   codebase="../classes
width=256 height=256>

suggests that there is a path called directory called classes where class files are stored. This class directory is one directory up from the HTML file, and the class we're looking for is the pool directory below motodave. If I had left the billiards class in the same directory as the HTML file, I could have written:

```
<applet code="billiards.class" width=256 height=256>
```

Primitive Data Types

Data types are the building blocks of a software program. A type, being the most basic structure, is all programmers had to work with before object-oriented languages, which built types into more complex objects, which could then be repurposed. We've ventured up the lineage from custom packages to the Java Class Libraries and looked at the **java.lang** package that wraps data types in objects. These packages are made up of classes constructed with Java primitive data types. We can presume that platform-dependent Java interpreters are built in a language other than Java (the old chicken and egg problem) and that they are built of data types.

The foundation of Java (the language, the compiler, the interpreter and the virtual machine specification) allows Java's implementation of primitive types to be very modern. Other high-level programming languages are not as specific or rigorous about how the types are implemented in terms of the size in bits and the range of values they can hold. This allows programmers in other languages to optimize a program for a particular architecture but makes it difficult to port the application to another operating system or hardware platform. Java takes away the uncertainty by requiring identical sizes and fixed ranges of the eight primitive data types on all platforms. Performance issues will be overcome by Just In Time (JIT) compilers that convert the byte-codes to machine-specific code at run time and perhaps dedicated hardware (Java Chips).

Logic Type

Boolean

Booleans are the simplest type. A boolean stores a value of true or false. Because binary data consists of zeros and ones, only one bit is needed to set a value of true or false, with 0 = false and 1 = true. Other types require 16 to 64 bits to convey all the information they store. Because in Java the boolean type is actually a value of true or false and nothing else (it is not 0 or 1, the integers), it cannot automatically be cast as an int type. In C and MOO, there are no actual values of "true" and "false," 0 is false and 1 is true, so you can cheat in C by freely using numbers as booleans and vice versa. For example, in C you can say "if (somenumber) then do a task, and pass if (somenumber) is 0." In Java, you would say "if variable myVar is equivalent to 10 then a boolean check to determine if it were 10 would come back true."

An example from the MOO is also useful in understanding the relationship of booleans and integers. In MOO, a length operator returns a number that is the length of an array or a list. If there are three items in a room, then the room's .contents property has those three items object numbers in a list. **length(here.contents)** would return 3. If I want my code to do something if there are any objects in the room, I can code it like this:

```
if (length(here.contents)

(do something with the contents))
endif
```

Because length (here.content) is not 0, the if statement passes. If there were something in the room, the if statement fails. So the boolean is implied by, or cast to, an integer.

In Java, the boolean type checks for 0 or null to return a statement as being false, so you would have to phrase it this way:

```
{if (length(here.contents) != 0)
    (do stuff)}
```

This does not restrict what you can do in Java, you just need to be aware of it if you are used to programming in C, so you don't go bonkers trying to figure out why your code won't work. Shortened forms of testing in an "if" statement used to be more important to get faster code, when programmers worried about every clock cycle. On the MOO, you need to be concerned about producing "spammy" or "laggy" code rather than elegant code.

The ImageMap program offers a good example of the use of the Java boolean type in action. This mouseExit() method goes through each ImageMapArea and in each determines if the mouse has exited (by setting areas[i].entered to false). It also checks to see if any of the areas were active and keeps track if they were. Then, it calls 'repaint()' to refresh the display if anything has changed (if the variable changed is now true, where it started with false) :

```
public void mouseExit() {
    boolean changed = false;

    for (int i = 0; i < areas.length; i++) {
        if (areas[i].active) {
            areas[i].entered = false;
            changed = true;
        }
    }
    if (changed) {
        repaint();
    }
}
```

Void in the first line means that method mouseExit() itself is not expected to return any value (see below). **changed** is a boolean type that is set to false. If any active area is entered by the mouse, that boolean type is changed to true. And when the value of true is returned, the repaint method is called.

type: **boolean**
contains: true/false
default: false
size: 1 bit

Language Type

char

A **char** contains a character, such as 'm'. You can have an array of characters, such as {m, o, u, s, e}, but this is not the same as a **string**, such as "mouse." In Java, the **char** type represents a character encoded according to the Unicode standard that defines the characters of all modern languages in two bytes (16 bits.) While most systems can still handle only ASCII and ISO8859 (Latin-1) characters, future systems with greater built-in font capability will benefit from an international language that natively speaks Unicode.

type: **char**
contains: Unicode value
default: /u000
size: 16bits
range: /u0000 to /uFFFF

Integral Arithmetic Types

A **byte**, as is known to most people who otherwise know nothing about computers, is composed of 8 bits (eight zeros or ones). It can hold a range of values from -128 to 127. It is beneficial to use the smallest type you can for a particular task, especially if large arrays are involved. If you have 50,000 employee records, saving 8 bytes per record by using **byte** rather than **short** will be significant. While the

Java virtual machine has built-in memory management (see Garbage Collection below), for disk space, speed, and general efficiency, there are four integer types in Java, rather than one big one.

byte
containssigned integer
default0
size8 bits
range-128 to 127

short
typesigned integer
default0
size16 bits
range-32768 to 32767

int
typesigned integer
default0
size32 bits
range-2147483648 to 2147483647

long
typesigned integer
default0
size64 bits
range-9223372036854775808 to 9223372036854775807

Floating Point Types

Floats and **doubles** do a lot internally that the programmer doesn't have to think about, or be aware of, to use. They store the mantissa, the sign, and the exponent. 3746578 e-3 means 3746.578, and **float** has fixed width fields for the 3746578 part (the mantissa), the - part (the sign) and the 3 part (the exponent). The calculation happens automatically; the programmer just needs to know that if you are trying to store a fractional number, a very small number or very large number, a float is needed. The bottom line is that **floats** store real numbers with decimal places. Java uses the IEEE standard for storing floats, the most commonly implemented in hardware, so that there is minimal (and fast) translation to any particular native machine environment or floating point math chip. It's been a while since any programmer had to deal directly with float internals. Any PC has floating point math operators right in the wires of the CPU, but knowing a little about what floats really are improves your overall grasp of which type is appropriate for a task

float
contains IEEE 754 floating-point
default   0.0
size   64 bits
range   +/-3.4E+38 to +/-1.4E-45 with 6 to 7 significant figures of accuracy

double
contains IEEE 754 floating-point
default   0.0
size   64 bits
range   +/-1.7E+308 to +/-4.9E-324 with 14 to 15 significant figures of accuracy

Build a Rocket, Send it to the Moon

- To understand how all these types fit together to make up objects, let's look at an example: programming a rocket ship.
- You make a variable to hold the number of stages on the rocket. For that you want a small integer. The type would be **byte**.
- It would need to store only 1 through 3 or 4. You would want a variable for the current speed, which would need a larger integer. Assuming it will break 128 miles per hour, you would use **short**.

85

- Then there are variables such as whether the fuel is burning (postignition) or still, whether the hatch is closed, whether the safety-belt is fastened. You'd make an EngineOn variable, a HatchClosed variable and a SafetyBeltFastened variable, all of type **boolean**. This will allow you to set requirements such as:

```
if  (hatchClosed && SafetyBeltFastened && !engineOn)
    ignite();
```

(if the hatch is closed and safety belts are fastened go ahead and ignite).You can have a very simple method for ignition. You ignite the rockets and it checks for whether the rockets are lit or not already, whether the belts are fastened, and whether the hatch is closed. If those cases are correct, that method would just set EngineOn to true.

```
void ignite() {
engineOn = true;
}
```

When the rocket is painted, the paint method can display fiery exhaust when the EngineOn is set to true and stillness with a few herons when EngineOn is set to false. One boolean on its own is simple, but a well-developed sequence of boolean switches and contacts, displayed with the AWT, could model the rocket's cockpit in detail. When you flip the final switch, you get launch.
- After launch, your **int** would handle altitude, and **long**, **float**, and **double** would model the trajectory, orbit and drift and analyze the neutrino content of deep space.
- **char** would place [U, ., ,S,., , A, ., ,] proudly on the side of the craft.

Void, the no-type type

Assume you had the method:

```
boolean big(int i) {
   if (i > 100) {
     return true;
   } else {
     return false;
   }
}
```

The "boolean" keyword means it will return a boolean value (return true, or return false). This method would be 'assigned' to a value, such as:

```
boolean b;
b = big(200)
```

But if you had:

```
void big() {
    System.out.println("Sooooo big!")
}
```

In this case, "void" is a stand in replacement for a primitive data type. It's the "none" data type. "Void" could just as easily be said to replace an "int" so as not to return an integer. But a method can return an Object as easily as it can return a primitive type. In this code snippet (from the AWT package API) getImage() returns an Image:

public Image getImage(URL url, String name);

The method getImage() returns an image object. If it stated void getImage(), rather than int getImage(), boolean getImage() or Image getImage(), it would not return an object or anything else.

CHAPTER 15   *A Field Guide to Java*

Java in its Natural Habitat

Rather than thinking abstractly about what java is, what it means, and what it can do, let's go out in the field and stalk a live Java applet, bag it, take it apart and see how it work. Then we can start to consider how we'll build our own.

The Field Kit

As a student of Javacology, you'll need

1. a laboratory setting in which to perform your experiments,
2. a vehicle to get to the field,
3. tools to collect and view specimens,
4. Petri dishes, greenhouses, and incubators in which to create new life,
5. and ultimately a journal in which to publish the results.

Fortunately for the armchair Javacologist, everything you need is probably sitting on your desk.

1. **A computer** that can run Java-based programs.

   In this book, we'll refer to this computer as your desktop computer or client computer, as opposed to the **Server** (below). Because Java is architecture-neutral, it should make little difference whether this computer runs Windows95, NT, UNIX (XWindows) or MacOS. Java is most likely built directly into the operating system. The examples will be based on a UNIX command-line environment, as the more "verbose" output will give you a better sense of what is happening than by doing everything with a graphic interface. It will be easy to transfer your understanding to your environment afterwards. We won't delve too deeply into these applications or using the Internet, as there are many good books available on the subject.

2. To begin, the applications you have loaded on your computer will need to include:

   FTP, TELNET, Wbb Browser, TCP/IP stack

   Any of these programs can be written in Java and will soon be available in Java packages, but it's better to get started with one developed for your platform.

FTP: File Transfer Protocol. Used for moving documents and binary, executable code between computers on the Internet. Your FTP client software should allow you to choose between Text (ASCII) or Graphics/Software (Binary) mode, depending on what you are transferring. It should also allow you to GET a file from another computer on the Internet, or to PUT a file on the remote computer, and to choose what directory (or folder) the file should go in.

You will be using FTP to move Java bytecode (executable programs), source code, graphics, audio files and HTML pages between your computer and the server. If we start with just FTP, we can use it to pull in the rest of the software we need. If you are starting with a truly clean slate, you can build up your suite of tools using only a modem and terminal software.

Here's an example:

- Connect to your Internet Service Provider (ISP) with Zterm or Win-Term (or whatever terminal emulator came with your modem).
- Use the FTP software that's on the ISP's host to transfer the FTP application for your platform. Fetch, an FTP program for the Mac, for example, can be FTP'd from DARTVAX.DARTMOUTH.EDU in the /pub directory. You can also use FTP to get a TCP/IP stack such as Trumpet Winsock (for Windows).
- Use sz command on the ISP host or Kermit to transfer the software to your client computer.
- Configure TCP/IP stack for your network (information should be provided by your ISP). If you have a dial-up connection, you will need PPP software that can also be found on the Net.
- Use FTP to get Telnet and a Web browser.

TELNET: Terminal Interface. Used for connecting to a remote computer on the network or across the Internet. With Telnet, you can launch applications on remote computers (also called hosts or servers) to:

- Write documents on the server or edit documents already moved to the server, such as HTML files or Java source code (pico, emacs, vi)
- Interact with other users (Talk, IRC or TinyFugue)
- Compile Java source code into bytecode (javac)
- Configure software on the server (Web server software, MOOs, databases)

Before direct Internet connections (such as PPP and digital connections; see below) that allow the use of Graphical User Interfaces (GUIs) became standard, a terminal interface was the way a remote user viewed the Internet. As you'll see, a lot was lost when Internet providers began shipping Web Browsers and e-mail packages as the standard Internet software. I consider this the great "dumbing down" of the Net, which was necessary for it to become a mass-market phenomenon. An awful lot of work can be done on a remote computer using Telnet, so you'll have to become familiar with it. Many service providers do not allow you to Telnet to the hosts where you are storing your content, as it's a "security risk," but require you to finish everything on your computer, and move it to the server with FTP. Having an Internet account with a UNIX Shell is a must for understanding all the possibilities of an Internet service if you don't have the luxury of having a UNIX box on your own network. Later in this work we'll write our own Telnet client in Java.

Web browser: HotJava or Netscape 2.0 or higher is currently required to participate in these experiments. The main reason we need Netscape or HotJava is that it will be our platform for launching "applets," small Java programs delivered to the browser from various locations around the Internet. The Java browser will be acting as our Java interpreter, taking the Java programs (bytecode) from a remote computer (server), checking them for errors and violations, and executing them on the client computer.

TCP/IP stack: Whether you are on a local area network with a direct digital connection to the Internet or using a modem connection, you will need a TCP/IP stack to address your computer on the Internet and run the applications listed above. If you are on a modem connection, you will need a PPP (Point to Point Protocol) dialer to make a direct TCP/IP connection over your telephone line.

3. A Network (or a connection to the Internet).

Java inhabits networks. It is designed to produce applications that communicate events between users on different computers across a network, to interpret those events, and to display the results of the user interaction. These events generally revolve around the typing of input on a keyboard, mouse movements, and clicks. In a live, multiuser application, the typing and the mouse-clicks are often in response to graphics, sounds and movements on the screen. These "events" are often caused by typing and mouse-clicks on a remote computer. In a "client-server" application, events are communicated by various remote clients, processed by a server, and new information messaged back to the clients. In some cases, the applications on the two client computers are communicating directly, as "peers." This is known as "peer-to-peer" communication.

The performance of your applications can be determined as much by the bandwidth (capacity) and timing (latency) of the network connections between computers as by the power of the computer running the applications.

New computers that reduce internal lag by using switches rather than buses and come complete with a high-capacity network interface card (NIC), the common deployment of high-bandwidth local and wide area networks, and the deployment by the phone and cable companies of fully-digital Internet data services to homes and small businesses, such as ISDN (Integrated Services Digital Network), ADSL (Asynchronous Digital Subscriber Line), and HDSL (High bit-rate Digital Subscriber Line) and the fiber/coaxial cable hybrids of the cable companies are all contributing to the increasing ability to transfer data at high speed. Whether the Internet backbone itself can keep up with the demand is yet to be seen. As new programs require ever greater computing power, new programs are also requiring greater network capacity. It will be a good idea to design your applications to be network efficient as well as memory efficient.

It is important to know about your local network or Internet connection and be aware that others have greater or lesser capacity than you. You can distribute the class files, graphics, audio and other files in advance using an FTP server, rather than loading them all over the network. You can also load classes dynamically after the user has begun working with the application. With new NCs on a fast local network, classes can be loaded from the server in the same time a standalone Windows application, such as Word, can be loaded on the desktop by a PC. Over PPP connections at 28.8 kilobits per seconds (Kpbs), users will often arrest a download rather than waiting for a large applet to be received.

4. A Java Interpreter

This is present in Netscape 2.0 and above and in the appletviewer that comes with JDK 1.0. You can also run Java applications from the command line if you have JDK installed on your computer. This is important to understand if developing for very stripped-down systems running little more than a small operating system and Java. Netscape is not necessary.

Soon, there will important performance questions involved with choosing a Java client environment. JIT (Just in Time) compilers will translate Java bytecode to native machine code on-the-fly as the class is loaded, making real-time Java applications possible. At present, the slowness of Java interpreters make real-time simulations and games ineffective.

5. A Java Development Environment (JDE)

The most important element of a JDE is the Java compiler, which we will use straight from the JDK. A JDE is generally more featureful and includes point-and-click access to all the classes and methods in the Java API. JDEs include Sun Microsystems's Java Workshop for Solaris, Symantec Cafe for Windows95, and Roaster for the Macintosh.

6. **A Server**

Your server can be the same computer as the client computer described above. Most modern systems are capable of running HTTP daemons, and can be hit by a browser as the localhost (IP address: 127.0.0.1 or by an Internet IP address). Whether your server is a shared computer provided by your ISP, a workstation on your corporate LAN or a dedicated system for your Internet publishing, its significance here is its role in storing class files before they are loaded by the browser or interpreter.

Field Notes

Make sure you have a good understanding of your operating environment. If you run into trouble and wind up sending me mail to complain that nothing works, or if you communicate with other Java programmers on the USENET newsgroup comp.lang.java, you should keep all these factors in mind as they will influence the performance of your applets and applications or the way you go about developing them.

_Client computer:______(hardware platform)

_____ (operating system)

_____ (processor and RAM)

_Applications:______(telnet client)

_____(ftp client)

_____(browser)

_____(IP Stack)

_Network:______(capacity to end-user/desktop)

_____(your connection)
_____(capacity to server)

_____(network protocols and services)

Java Interpreter:_____

Development Kit:_____

_Server:______(hardware platform)

_____(operating system)

_____(processor and RAM)

Anatomy of a URL

URL, or Universal Resource Locator, is the naming convention that uniquely identifies each service and file on the Internet. While the Web has been called a poor man's distributed object computing environment, its ability to include Java classes among the data objects that can be accessed makes it much richer.

A URL can be broken down as follows:

```
protocol://host.domain.service:port/directory/subdirec-
tory/filename.type
```

For example:

- news://spy.lab.com:563/butterfly.mb, if entered in your Netscape browser, will use NNTP (Network News Transfer Protocol) to enter port 563 on a host known as "spy" in the "lab" domain on the "com" network set aside for commercial services. The newsgroup you will access will be for the discussion of the MoonBean protocol
- telnet://lambda.parc.xerox.com:8888 would launch a Telnet client to log you into MOO running on port 8888 of lambda, a computer at Xerox PARC, a commercial service.
- ftp://ftp.netscape.com will log you into Netscape's anonymous FTP server to download the latest version of their browser software.
- and http://www.butterfly.net/motodave/zoe.gif will send you a nice photograph of my daughter Zoe that's located in my public directory on our Web server. The .gif extension is the MIME-type, which, if you're using the default selection on your helper-applications, should load in the browser. http://www.butterfly.net/moto-dave/zoe.html will send you the whole file with a lot more interesting information about Zoe.

## CHAPTER 16

Java: A Children's Tale

The only way to learn a programming language is to begin using it. As in learning a foreign language, you need to do the exercises, listen to the teacher and recite the dialogues with your classmates. But it doesn't have to be painful. I like to view the creation of an application (or an applet) in Java in the framework of the children's story *Stone Soup*.

Stone Soup

In this book, if I recall correctly, a tattered stranger comes to town, and asks the locals if they can spare some food. He is told there is not enough food in the town to share. He tells the townspeople that to make a great feast, all he will need is a stone. If someone from the town can bring him a stone, he will make a nutritious and delicious soup for everyone. When the stone arrives, he says he will need a big pot to cook it in. So someone brings him a pot.

Then, he says, we need some water to boil the stone and wood for the fire to heat the water. When the stone is boiling, the stranger announces that we just need some carrots. Does anyone have some carrots for the stone soup? Carrots are found and added to the pot. After a bit he tastes the soup. Hmmm, he says, pretty good, but it needs some pepper. Someone brings pepper. Now, said the stranger, all it needs is some cabbage and maybe a ham bone. Cabbage and a ham bone are found. This pattern continues until a wonderful soup is made that feeds the entire village.

StoneSoup

The Stone (Creating an Object)

Programming in Java is very similar to making stone soup.

First, you ask for an Object.

```
import java.lang.Object
```

Any object you need can be derived from the Object class.

```
class StoneSoup extends java.lang.Object
```

This is your first program in Java. It is your first real source code. If you wanted to comment it (you should always comment your code, so you can read it later and understand what you were thinking), it would say:

```
/*
 * This is motodave's first attempt at writing java.
 * all I have done so far is to define a class, StoneSoup,
 * which is nothing yet, except that it is descended from
 * Object, so it inherits all the properties of Object. The
 * townsfolk have already started bringing me things.
 */
//if you only have a short comment you can use this style
```

```
/** this type of comment will help produce documentation */
class StoneSoup extends java.lang.Object
```

Once we have our stone we have to put it somewhere. You might have jotted down our stone code in the Notepad function on your PC, or you might have written it in Word or WordPerfect, or you have thought ahead and waited to find out the appropriate place to write this code. Anyway, it's not yet written in stone. Save this file as plain ASCII text. Save it as **stone.java**.

Because this will eventually become an applet, it should reside on a Web server so you can deliver it with a Web page and allow it to execute on the user's system. You have the option of creating the applet on your desktop computer system and then transferring the applet to your Web server using FTP (File Transfer Protocol) (see above), or you can remotely log onto the Web server (using Telnet) and write and compile your applet there. For the purposes of this exercise, we will use the latter method. This way, we can create Java-based Internet services, use them, debug them, and build on them at the same time.

To produce our bytecode, we're going to use Sun's Java Development Kit (JDK) 1.0. There are many more fully featured development environments, but it's good to understand how the basic systems work before you choose which one most suits your long-term needs.

The Town Square (Putting it on the Web server)

As we've said, we need a place to put the stone and to add all the other ingredients. A place to cook the soup and ultimately serve it from. Where do we put the pot? Your Internet Service Provider (ISP) is one option and is in many ways a town square. Many providers give users accounts on systems that are running Web servers. The majority of these systems are run on a flavor of UNIX. At HuskyLabs, we run Solaris on SPARCstatiosn and UltraSPARCs from Sun Microsystems. Let's imagine your ISP runs UNIX and has a standard Web server configuration that allows you to put files in your home directory. Also, make sure your ISP will give you a shell account. It's a lot easier to update your Web site if you have shell access, not just a PPP connection. If you have Internet connectivity through your business or school, find out about getting a shell account on a UNIX host.

We are working on MONARCH (the name of our Java Production station) and only need to move the file to IRON.

On your system, you might have a graphic Telnet application, but we'll do things from a command line. If you understand the commands, you can figure out what to enter into the fields of your Telnet client. (Later, we'll write our own Telnet client with Java and build it into a Web page.)

```
/export/home/motodave% telnet iron
Trying 206.102.92.2 ...
Connected to iron.butterfly.net.
Escape character is '^]'.
UNIX(r) System V Release 4.0 (iron)
login: motodave
Password:
Last login: Mon Feb 19 12:16:56 from monarch.butterfly.net
Sun Microsystems Inc.   SunOS 5.5       Generic November 1995
         Welcome to HuskyLabs, Shepherdstown, West Virginia
1:24pm up 1 day, 18:22, 7 users,load average: 0.94, 0.96, 1.00
You have mail.
/opt/home/motodave%
```

Now we create a directory for our public files, which is by convention called public_html. You'll need to find out from your system administrator which it is. We'll think of this directory as the Town Square.

Go ahead and type: mkdir public_html.

```
/opt/home/motodave 52% mkdir public_html
```

Now if you list the files in your directory, you'll see that you created a directory called public_html. Now list the files, and make sure it's there.

```
/opt/home/motodave% ls
/opt/home/motodave% public_html
```

Now we'll enter the public square.

```
/opt/home/motodave% cd pub_html
/opt/home/motodave/pub_html%
```

Let's look around (by using the list command (ls)):

```
/opt/home/motodave/public_html% ls
/opt/home/motodave/public_html%
```

There's nothing there. Let's get the kettle.

The Kettle (Creating the Web page)

Because we're working in code, we don't have to go very far to get a kettle to contain our applet soup. We just make one. The kettle will be an HTML file that will serve up our applet. We'll use the vi editor, which is complicated to use but ultimately very powerful. Eventually, when you're a code warrior, you'll also want to be a vi trooper, so we might as well get started. If your ISP has pico on the server, you might want to try that first (type "pico kettle.html" instead of "vi kettle.html and follow the editing instructions on the screen).

```
/opt/home/motodave/public_html% vi kettle.html
```

You'll see a screen of ~ (tildes) and the words: "kettle.html" [New file] at the bottom of your screen. The vi editor has two modes, an edit mode and an insert mode. When you initiate vi, it's by default in the editor mode. You need to switch to the insert mode by typing a lowercase "i." The only thing we have to decide is how big you want the kettle to be. Let's say there are 100 people in the town, so we'll make it big enough to serve 100. Let's create the HTML kettle that will serve up your applet. Again, even in HTML, we can use comments in the text so we understand later what we were trying to do. In HTML, comments are delimited by <!--comment --> Type:

```
<HTML>
<HEAD>
<TITLE>Stone Soup</TITLE>
</HEAD>
<!--Let's make the Kettle black, by setting the bgcolor -->
<!--Writing comments in HTML is different than in Java-->
<body bgcolor="#000000" text="#ff4500" link="ffff00"
vlink="fff000">
<P>
Here is my first applet: Stone Soup
</P>
<applet code = "StoneSoup" width =400 height =40>
<applet>
```

Then save the file. First you have to go into edit mode by hitting the *esc* key. Then type *:wq* for "command: write, quit."

Type *ls* on the command line, which will show you that you do indeed have a kettle (kettle.html) in the Town Square (pub_html).

Now let's put the stone in the pot. We'll move it from the desktop machine to the server, using File Transfer Protocol (FTP).

```
/export/home/motodave% ftp
ftp> open iron
Connected to iron.butterfly.net.
220 iron FTP server (UNIX(r) System V Release 4.0) ready.
Name (iron:motodave):
331 Password required for motodave.
Password:
230 User motodave logged in.
ftp> cd pub_html
250 CWD command successful.
ftp> put stone.java
```

Gathering Wood (Getting a developer's environment)

Now that we have both the source code, from which all else will spring **(stone.java)**, and the document or container **(kettle.html)** in the public square (on the server, IRON, in our public directory), step back and take look at the **Kettle** in your browser. To do this, launch Netscape and open the URL **http://www.butterfly.net/~motodave/ kettle.html**; you'll see a black page with the words: "Here is my first applet: Stone Soup" in white letters, with a box below it, 100 pixels by 100 pixels square, reserved for your applet. But there is no applet yet. All we have is source code, not byte code, which are binary files that can be interpreted by the Java-enabled browser.

We realize we don't have all the tools yet. We need to gather some wood, get an axe, and some matches, so we can cook our stone and make some soup. It's getting late and I'm sure you're getting hungry. All the implements for making the fire are located on the Web, at Sun Microsystem's Javasoft site. Follow the links from **http://www.java-soft.com** to the Java Developer's Kit. I got there by clicking on Downloading, then selecting the link to the Java Developer's Kit I wind up at: **http://www.javasoft.com/JDK-1.0/index.html**. When we get deep enough, we find that the best way to get the software is by FTP, rather than HTTP. Before, we used the FTP "Put" command to move the stone.java file from our home computer to the Web server out on the Net. Before, we transferred a text file in ASCII mode to the server, now we will download an application in Binary mode. You can use FTP to pull files all the way to your home computer or to move them between Internet servers. Since we're working on a server that runs Solaris and is connected over high-capacity lines to the Net, we'll just download the file from Javasoft to your home directory on IRON.

```
/opt/home/motodave% ftp ftp.javasoft.com
Name (ftp.javasoft.com): anonymous
331 Guest login ok, send your complete e-mail address as
  password.
```

```
Password: motodave@butterfly.net
<< informational messages <<
ftp> binary
200 Type set to I.
ftp> cd pub
<< more informational messages <<
250 CWD command successful.
ftp> get JDK-1_0-solaris2-sparc.tar.Z
200 PORT command successful.
150 Opening BINARY mode data connection for JDK-1_0-solaris2-
  sparc.tar.Z (4595974 bytes).
226 Transfer complete.
local: JDK-1_0-solaris2-sparc.tar.Z remote: JDK-1_0-solaris2-
  sparc.tar.Z
4595974 bytes received in 1.4e+02 seconds (30 Kbytes/s)
ftp> bye
```

Now that you've collected the wood, you have to chop it up. The Java Developer's Kit (JDK) for Solaris is in a Tape Archive (.tar) that is compressed (Z). Uncompress it by typing:

```
/opt/home/motodave/ uncompress JDK (Esc)
```

When you type the "escape" key, UNIX will fill in the rest of the string. When you press return, you will have the file uncompressed and will have to untar it. Type:

```
/opt/home/motodave/ tar -xvf JDK (Esc)
```

This will extract (x) the file (f) in verbose mode (v) and create a directory beneath your home directory called "java." There will be a lot of useful good tools, such as the appletviewer, sample applets and source material packed in the JDK, but we'll concern ourselves for now with the **Flint & Steel**, the java compiler.

Lighting the Fire (Compiling)

We're just about ready to strike the flame and cook up our java source code into a binary applet. You need to set your path so that the directory $HOME/java/bin is found when you type the command to execute the java compiler. You're still in your home directory, where you unpacked the JDK, so type.

```
set path=($path $HOME/java/bin)
```

This will preserve your current paths that give you access to the software on this Server and add a path so that you can invoke the java compiler (located under your home directory in java/bin (for binary's) from any directory on the system.

Now in our Public Directory (the Town Square), we have two files in human readable form, the kettle.html and the stone.java. We need to light the fire and cook the stone into our tasty soup. To do this, type:

```
/opt/home/motodave/public_html% javac StoneSoup.java
```

Look in the directory again, and you'll see that another file has automagically appeared.

```
/opt/home/motodave/public_html% ls
StoneSoup.class     kettle.html    StoneSoup.java
```

StoneSoup.class is a file of java bytecodes that the compiler (javac) produced from the source code. Javac didn't give us any errors when we compiled it, so it must not have found anything too offensive. So let's look at it in Netscape (our browser/java interpreter). Hit reload, but make sure you've set the cache to 0, so we make sure it pulls in the new page, and you'll see: nothing. You have a program that compiled, but not featureful. All you have done so far is to define a class, called StoneSoup, and compiled it. There are no behaviors, no attributes, no methods or variables. In fact, it's instantiated as an object, it's still only a template.

Where did the stone come from? From what did it derive its properties?

First, we know that StoneSoup is an applet (so that we can serve it up to the world from our kettle). Let's ask our neighbors if someone can contribute applet properties to our StoneSoup. One way we can do this is to state that:

```
class StoneSoup extends java.applet.Applet
```

This means we will take the class Applet from the **class library** (or **package)** java.applet.* In fact, we might guess that there are other classes in the class library besides Applet that would be useful in this project. So let's bring in the whole kit and caboodle. This will allow us to just call classes in the library by name, and the compiler will know where to look for them.

```
//StoneSoup.java
import java.applet.*
class StoneSoup extends Applet
```

We try a quick compile on this source code and get an error: looks like a bug has crawled into the soup!

```
/opt/home/motodave/public_html 82% javac StoneSoup.java
StoneSoup.java:1: ';' expected.
import java.applet.*
                   ^
StoneSoup.java:2: Superclass Applet of class StoneSoup not
    found.
class StoneSoup extends Applet
      ^
2 errors
```

This is one level of debugging... looking at errors from the compiler. Let's fix the error, which is syntactical. The compiler expected a semicolon, so we'll give it one. This will wind up taking care of both errors. When the java.applet.* package was not imported correctly, it was not able to find the Applet class, from which we've told the compiler StoneSoup was derived. With the semicolon, the program will compile correctly.

```
//StoneSoup.java
import java.applet.*;
class StoneSoup extends Applet
```

Now we can recompile and, seeing no errors, move to the second part of the debugging process. Using Netscape 2.0 as your applet-viewer, select "Show Java Console" from the options menu. A window will appear that will let you know the state of any applets that might have been downloaded with the page. Make sure the cache is set to zero on the Netscape Navigator, so that you are loading a new page, not reloading the one that is cached locally on your computer. This can be done by selecting Options on the toolbar, Network Preferences, then Cache. Set Memory and Disk Cache to zero, and press Clear Memory Cache Now and Clear Disk Cache Now. Then reload the page.

This is the error we get in the Java Console window:

```
# Applet exception: class StoneSoup was not constructed
  properly
java.lang.IllegalAccessException: StoneSoup
at netscape.applet.EmbeddedAppletFrame.run(EmbeddedApplet
  Frame.java:230)
at java.lang.Thread.run(Thread.java:289)
```

It's hard to tell from this cryptic note how it was improperly constructed. So we turn to a tool that came with the JDK, the applet-viewer. The appletviewer is like a browser, but it does not display the whole Web page, only the portion defined within the <APPLET> tag. There is an actual debugger provided with the JDK and most Java Development Environments, but we have enough information here to move forward. With the appletviewer we see:

```
load: StoneSoup is not public or has no public constructor
```

We're asking the townspeople for a lot in terms of ingredients for our soup, and we've promised, in turn, to make the soup public. It turns out we need to declare the StoneSoup class public for it to be used by the interpreter. In the Java console, we saw an **IllegalAccessException** when Netscape tried to read the code and run it. Let's declare the class public and try again. Also, since we know that this is going to be an applet, we may as well state it up-front. The **java.lang.*** package is implicitly imported, thus accessible, regardless.

```
//StoneSoup.java
import java.applet.*;
public class StoneSoup extends Applet
```

This time, the applet compiles without complaint. When Netscape is run, there is a sign at the bottom of the window that "Applet Stone-Soup running." We see this whenever we move our mouse pointer over the field in the Navigator reserved for the applet.

## CHAPTER 17

Event-Driven Java

Since we have our tools, let's go out on the Net, get an applet with the source code, pull it apart, and see what makes it tick. The first we'll look at is called Eyecon, an applet written by Matthew Ross Davis that provides an interactive button on a Web page.

`http://www.lab.com/livejava/developers/eyecon.html`

An example of Eyecon, with a link to the source code, is at http://www.lab.com/livejava/developers/eyecon.html. Because we have our Stone still cooking in the pot, let's add some features and see if can't turn it into soup.

```
//StoneSoup.java
import java.applet.*;
public class StoneSoup extends Applet
```

First thing we need to do is change the name. Let's rename the public class Eyecon. The initial public class needs to have the same name as the file, so we'll call that Eyecon.java. If we don't, we will get the error:

```
/export/home/motodave% javac StoneSoup.java
StoneSoup.java:48: Warning: Public class Eyecon must be
```

```
defined in a file called "Eyecon.java".
public class Eyecon extends java.applet.Applet {
                     ^
```

So our new source code looks like:

```
//Eyecon.java
import java.applet.*;
public class Eyecon extends Applet
```

The idea of the Eyecon applet is that it will react to events triggered by mouse movements. First, an image is displayed. This appears to be a regular icon. When the mouse is moved over the icon, it changes to a new image and it makes a sound. When the mouse button is pressed, it changes again and makes a new sound. When the mouse button is released, it changes a final time, issues one last sound, and loads into the browser a new Web page.

This applet is simple to an experienced programmer but ambitious to the layman. Let's start by having the applet simply load the first image to set up the icon.

First, we'll edit the HTML page to reflect our new purpose. We need four graphics and four audio files to be loaded. We also need to specify the Web page that the interactive icon is to link to. By determining these in the applet parameters, we can reuse the Java applet on many pages by changing the HTML to call for different sound, images and link.

```
<HTML>
<HEAD>
<TITLE>Eyecon Demonstration</TITLE>
</HEAD>

<applet code = "Eyecon" width =40 height =40>
<!--The first parameter loads the startup gif-->
<param name="img1" value="images/guitar.gif">
<!--The second gif loads when the mouse enters-->
<param name="img2" value="images/jukebox.gif">
<!--The third loads when the mouse button goes down-->
```

```
<param name="img3" value="images/computer.gif">
<!--The fourth loads when the mouse button is released-->
<param name="img4" value="images/paymaster.gif">
<!--The first audio file plays when the mouse exits-->
<!--the image without clicking-->
<param name="snd1" value="audio/songbird.au">
<!--The second plays when the mouse enters the image-->
<param name="snd2" value="audio/crow.au">
<!-The third plays when the mouse button is pressed-->
<param name="snd4" value="audio/owl.au">
<!--The last plays when the mouse button is released-->
<param name="snd4" value-"audio/dove.au">
<!--The final parameter loads the next page-->
<param name="URL" value="http://www.butterfly.net/">
</applet>
</BODY>
</HTML>
```

On the Java coding side, let's start simple. Our applet should begin by reading from the first parameter what image is to be loaded, then displaying that image. Let's see if we can get that to work. Besides the Applet class, we know we'll need the Abstract Window Toolkit (AWT) package, so we should import that, too. **java.lang** is always available when Java is used, so we access to classes like String and Thread and the primitive type wrappers automatically.

All custom-built applets are created as subclasses of the Applet class, thereby inheriting the methods of the Applet class, which should then be overridden by your particular applet. These methods are called when needed by the Web browser or appletviewer. Two of the methods in the Applet package that we can use right away are getApplet-Info() and getParameterInfo().

>**java.applet.Applet.getAppletInfo()** returns information about the applet's author, copyright, version, and any other information the author wishes to provide.

>**java.applet.Applet.getParameterInfo()** returns the name, type and description of the applet resource elements defined in the Web page. These are passed to the applet as a three-element array of strings.

Other methods in the Applet class that do not need to be called but will be overridden as necessary include:

init(), which should be used to set variables to initial values (such as putting all the billiard balls in the rack in the pool example).

start(), which begins a thread that runs the main applet code.

stop(), arrests the applet.

destroy(), lets go of system resources the applet is holding.

Other Applet methods we'll be using in this example will include **getAudioClip()** and **getImage()**.

java.awt.Image The AWT enables much of Java's cross-platform compatibility. By defining its own GUI components, graphics controls, and layout managers, Java doesn't have to be dependent on any particular operating system. For example, Java doesn't know the difference between one OS's scrollbar and another's, it only knows scrollbar. The Java interpreter takes care of platform-dependent issues such as this. Nearly all Java applets use part of the java.awt package. Eyecon uses two particular classes in java.awt: Image and MediaTracker. While building Eyecon, we'll use the first of these, Image.

The Image class is an example of an abstract class. The whole idea behind having abstract classes is that they aren't actually able to do anything by themselves. They act as a data type in Java code and can be defined, initiated, and assigned compatible values just like primitive data types (int, long, float, double, etc.). The objects created from the Image class in Eyecon contain the GIF files to be displayed.

First, let's just grap the image and present it. This is a working applet that will take the first image listed in the parameters above and display it. To use this to display a different graphic, all you would have to do is change the value of "guitar.gif" to "saxaphone.gif" or whatever you wanted to display. The value of setting parameters is that you do not need to alter the source code and recompile to repurpose your applet.

```
 1. //DisplayImage.java is the file. Code by motodave.
 2. import java.applet.*;
 3. import java.awt.*;
 4. public class DisplayImage extends Applet {
 5. Image im1;
 6.public void init ()
 7.{  im1 = getImage (getCodeBase(), "guitar.gif");
 8.    resize(40, 40);
 9.}
10.public void paint(Graphics g)
11.{  g.drawImage(im1);
12.}
13.}
```

Line by Line

1. Comments in a simplified, on-line format. This is telling you that the source-code file is DisplayImage.java (as it should be since DisplayImage is the public class). I coded this as a simplified example of Matt's Eyecon applet. If this were a more impressive code specimen, I would comment more extensively within the code.
   1. //DisplayImage.java is the file. Code by motodave.

2. I know that I will need to use classes and methods in the **java.applet** package. I import the whole package so that I can refer to classes within it by their short name.
   2. import java.applet.*;

3. I also import java.awt.* for the same reason.
   3. import java.awt.*;

4. I name my custom-built class DisplayImage, the same name as the .java source file. I declare it public so that it can be accessed by the run-time system (the browser or appletviewer). I declare it to be a subclass (child) of java.applet.Applet so that it will inherit Applet's properties and those of applet's parent(s), in this case java.lang.Object. I open the brackets to define this class.
   4. public class DisplayImage extends Applet {

5. I create an object called im1, that is an instance of the abstract class Image (fullname: java.awt.Image).

5. Image im1;

6. Because our Class is public (so that it can be run as an applet, as described above), all the methods in our class have to be public. There are three methods in the java.applet.Applet class that will be introduced. The first appears in this line, init(). When an applet first runs and it needs to do something at the start, you put it in init(). In this case, that will be resize(). "Void" means that the method is not expected to return any value that can be assigned to a variable. It acts more like a "procedure" than a "function" as described above.

6. public void init ()

7. Inside the init() method, im1 is initialized to an image called "guitar.gif," which exists on the server in the same directory as the class file. If I had wanted the .gif in the same directory as the .html, I could have used getDocumentBase(). getCodeBase(), getDocumentBase() and getImage() are all methods of java.applet.Applet. getCodeBase() is used here in the list of parameters for getImage(URL *url*, String *name*);. The URL is set to whatever directory is pulled from codebase in the <APPLET> tag of the .html file received by the browser. "guitar.gif" is a String that matches the file name to be pulled residing in that directory. The value of im1 (the object) is set to the image that is pulled in from the server.

7. {im1 = getImage (getCodeBase(), "guitar.gif");

8. By default the applet area is small [Component.resize()], and resize() overrides this with parameters supplied by the author. In this case, I pass it two integers that match the pixel size of the graphic. resize(int *width*, int *height*).

8. resize(40, 40);

9. Closed bracket closes off the first method of Image im1.

9. }

10. Paint is another method of the Applet class that needs to be overridden. It is public because the applet itself is, and if you try to

override it with a protected or restricted method you'll get a compiler error. Paint is called automatically after start(). By default, paint() doesn't do anything but create the space. By overriding paint(), you define what should be drawn, in this case the single argument (Graphics g). The Graphics class provides methods for rendering lines, curves, colors, strings, drawings and images.
10.public void paint(Graphics g)

11. Here we tell the Graphics object that the behavior of paint() will be to draw the image defined above (that was "gotten" from the server).
11.{g.drawImage(im1);

12. This method is closed.
12.}

13. The class is closed.
13.}

Look into the Screen

Fire up your Java-enabled Web browser. Point it to **http:// www.lab.com/LiveJava/developers/phenomenon.html**. What happened?

`http://www.lab.com/LiveJava/developers/phenomenon.html`

The image of a butterfly emerges from the black backdrop. It flutters its wings as if it has alit, only momentarily, on your screen. Because the applet that rotates the butterfly images (producing the affect of animation) is powered by your own computer CPU, the rhythm of the wings fluctuates with the availability of system resources, bringing the butterfly to life.

Music starts. The first few bars of a cello solo dance to the rhythm of the butterfly's wings. It doesn't matter what kind of computer you are using, or what file format I chose for the sound, or whether you have a particular application on your computer. If you have a Java interpreter, such as Netscape, the song will play.

Buds appear in each corner. Move your mouse over one. A sound—birds twittering—indicates that the mouse arrow has entered the bud's field, and it blooms. An applet that was delivered to your computer with the text, graphics, and audio files has noted the mouse event and responded according to instructions embedded in the Web page. Press the mouse button. A new document is sent down the pipe and displayed on your desk.

Second Glance

The next page that comes up looks more like a traditional Web page. It seems kind of silly saying "traditional Web page," like the Web is something that's been around since the time of Homer, and Java is a modernist Joyce out to turn the art form on its distributed ear. But in a sense it's true. In our accelerated culture, The Web very quickly came to represent the co-opting of the Internet by corporate marketing teams, the erecting in cyberspace of the late capitalisms' cultural establishment. A hegemony that Java will overthrow. You can see the seeds of it in this page.

Move your mouse over the pyramid. It changes to a square. Why is this so revolutionary? Because I've invaded your space. Established contact. I did not send you a harmless Web page, but one embedded with a living object that responded to your touch.

Before Java, the Web was safe. The only two things your Browser could do was GET and POST, according to the specifications of the protocol HTTP (hypertext transfer protocol). When you entered a URL or selected a link, a request was sent for the particular document represented by the location. This was very convenient, if you wanted a static, distributed archive of documents.

Eyecon, Earcon

We started with the simple graphic displayer. Now we'll demonstrate a simple audio player. Then we'll put them together. Here's the <APPLET> tag of an HTML file for a page that plays a sound:

```
<applet code="AudioAuto.class" CODEBASE="/beta"
        width=2
        height=2>
<param name="file" value="/audio/ic.au">
</applet>
```

A major new feature is the java.applet.AudioClip class. Java natively supports 8-bit .au files at this point, but the options will improve.

java.applet.AudioClip Another item found in the java.applet package is the interface that enables us to deal with audio files, AudioClip. An interface such as this becomes a data type in actual code which can be assigned a value compatible with that data type (in this case, an audio file). As described above, this one will enable us to play, stop, and loop an audio file, using the play(), stop() and loop() methods. AudioClip is an abstract interface and, like an abstract class, cannot be instantiated, only used as a data type. In fact, all interfaces are inherently abstract. We don't have to implement this interface in our applet because it is already contained in java.applet.Applet.

java.lang.Thread This is a good example of scheduling thread s, as there is only one thread that stops or starts. The Thread class is instantiated in rockon, so that when Thread's run() method is invoked, rockon has a value that is not null, and the sound is played. If this wasn't done, the sound could continue when the browser leaves the page, running in a thread that is independent of the stopping and starting of the applet by the browser.

Here is the Java source:

```
/*
 * @(#)AudioAuto.java
```

```
         *
         * Copyright (c) 1995 HuskyLabs, Inc. All Rights Reserved.
         *
         * mozart@butterfly.net
         *
         * This is a very rudimentary applet that will play
         * a sound file as soon as its thread is started
         *
         */

        // Don't really need the AWT. We just import 2 classes.
        // by default we have access to java.lang.*, including
        //    String
        // we could have done the same thing with import
        //    java.applet.*
        import java.applet.Applet;
        import java.applet.AudioClip;

        //Runnable is an interface that lets us use threads
        public class AudioAuto extends Applet implements Runnable
          {

        // Applet info, displayed by some browsers
        public String getAppletInfo() {
        return "AudioAuto.java from HuskyLabs";
        }

        // tells the applet the name and location of the audio
        //    file
        public String[][] getParameterInfo() {
        String[][] info = {
        {"file", "string", "the name of the sound file"},
        };
        return info;
        }

        // The thread playing the sound, null is the default
        //    variable
        // for all reference variables. null is never cast to a
        // primitive type, such as boolean or int. It should not be
        // considered equal to zero unless it is specified.
        Thread rockon = null;
```

```
// an object "soundz" of class "AudioClip"
// [java.applet.AudioClip]
AudioClip soundz = null;

// this string holds the name of the audio file to play. An
// instantiation of java.lang.String as the musicFile
//    object.
String musicFile;

public void init() {
// For some reason, this assignment must be within a
//    method.
// It gets the name of the file from the html tag.
musicFile = getParameter("file");

// load the clip into the music object
if (soundz == null) {
soundz = getAudioClip(getCodeBase(), musicFile);
}
}

//run() is a method of java.lang.Thread
public void run() {
// set scheduling for the thread
Thread.currentThread().setPriority(Thread.NORM_PRIORITY-1);

// when the thread is running, do this
if (rockon != null) {
soundz.play();
} else {
soundz.stop();
}
}

// at start(), start up the thread
public void start() {
if (rockon == null) {
rockon = new Thread(this);
rockon.start();
}
}
```

```
// at stop(), shut down the thread
public void stop() {
if (rockon != null) {
rockon.stop();
rockon = null;
```

The Boolean Graphic, The Boolean Sound

Moving from painting a graphic on the screen to making an user-engaging interactive applet is really a very small step. If certain criteria are met (the mouse is within the applet frame, the mouse has left the frame, the mouse button is down, the mouse button is released), the Image will be instantiated in an incarnation, the AudioClip will be objectified in a different instance. The beauty comes in the tactile nature of the interaction. The rhythm that is created when the mouse moves over and out of the applet space is guided by the user. The desktop becomes an instrument, rather than a recording. We constructed a DisplayImage applet, which drew a simple graphic on the screen, and we built independently an AudioAuto applet that plays a sound when a thread is initiated and stops it when the thread is stopped. Now, to build our first, simple version of Eyecon, we can add a boolean that understands whether or not the mouse is in the image field and create a basic interactive button.

java.awt.Component and **java.awt.Event** Activity on the end user's computer can be captured in variables contained by the Event class. Methods in the Component class, such as mouseDown(), mouseUp(), mouseEnter(), mouseExit(), keyUp(), keyDown(), mouseDrag() and mouseMove() handle events on the desktop. Event contains instance variables that describe some activity on the GUI. When the methods of Component are called, the event handler passes the parameters for the location of the event to the objects and methods that require them.

This applet is considered version 1.0 because it doesn't really do anything. It offers interactivity, but an icon on a desktop should theoretically do something when selected and clicked. When this version of the icon is compiled, it produces one file called Ayecon.class.

```
Ayecon.java
/*
 * @(#)Ayecon.java v1.0
 *
 * Copyright (c) 1995 HuskyLabs, Inc. All Rights Reserved.
 *
 * mozart@butterfly.net
 *
 * This is a simple interactive icon
 *
 */


//These are the same packages used in DisplayImage
//java.applet also contains AudioClip
import java.applet.*;
import java.awt.*;

//Implements the Runnable interface to use the run() method
     of
//Threads
public class Ayecon extends Applet implements Runnable {

// mouse within? Sets a variable to the boolean type (T/F)
boolean within;

// The thread playing the sound
Thread imgThread = null;

// an object "im" of class "Image"
Image im = null;

// applet dimensions
final int appletWidth = 72;
final int appletHeight = 71;

String imgFile1, imgFile2, currentImage;

public void init() {
```

```
resize(appletWidth, appletHeight);

// For some reason, this assignment must be within a method
//  it gets the name of the file from the html tag
imgFile1 = getParameter("file1");
imgFile2 = getParameter("file2");

// load the graphics file into the object
if (im == null) {
im = getImage(getCodeBase(), imgFile1);
}
}

public void run() {
// set scheduling for the thread
Thread.currentThread().setPriority(Thread.NORM_PRIORITY-1);

// when the thread is running, do this
if (imgThread != null) {
repaint();
}
}

// attempt to capture a mouse event
public boolean mouseDown(java.awt.Event event, int x,
  int y) {
return true;
}

// mouse enter!!!
public boolean mouseEnter(java.awt.Event event, int x,
  int y) {
im = getImage(getCodeBase(), imgFile2);
repaint();
return true;
}

// mouse exit!!!
public boolean mouseExit(java.awt.Event event, int x,
  int y) {
im = getImage(getCodeBase(), imgFile1);
repaint();
return true;
}
```

```
// painting: parameters are the (object, x/y coordinates of
// the mouse location, and this, the current object
public void paint(Graphics g) {
g.drawImage(im, 0, 0, this);
}

// update
public void update(Graphics g) {
paint(g);
}

// at start(), start up the thread
public void start() {
if (imgThread == null) {
imgThread = new Thread(this);
imgThread.start();
}
}

// at stop(), shut down the thread
public void stop() {
if (imgThread != null) {
imgThread.stop();
imgThread = null;
}
}
}
```

Now we're ready to move to a full-featured applet. The big difference between Ayecon and Eyecon is that the latter does not just provide empty feedback to the user, but will fetch another Web page if clicked. The difference between a Java-enabled button such as Eyecon and a standard .gif image that is linked to is that the user can be made to expect a certain occurence, or gain information and context before an event is triggered by a mouse click.

For example, in computer-based training, or in children's activities, an icon can prompt vocally, "when you press the mouse button, you will enter the gray zone." The user can then decide if that is what they were hoping to do, rather than guessing from a one-word tag or the context of an image. Pull-down menus are a staple of interface design to organize deeper levels of content. A scrollbar offers the possibility of a single icon to reference multiple URLs without imagemapping. When Eyecon.java is compiled, two .class files are produced: Eyecon.class and Linkme.class. Eyecon performs the user interface functions, and Linkme fetches the new URL.

java.net.URL This class allows a page referenced by a URL to be fetched across the network and displayed in the browser. The URL can be a single string or a list of separate protocol, host, port, and file names. Once the parameter is handled, you'll see it's very easy to link to another page.

Exceptions If an address is not properly constructed, a MalformedURLException will be thrown. If an exception is thrown, it can be caught and handled gracefully, so that the program continues to be useful after the error condition occurs. Provisions should be made for diverting the program down a path of recovery so that it can be handled without heading down the same path again, which will cause the program to cease. Exceptions can be thrown purposefully, with throw [Exception], with [Exception] being an object that instantiates a child of java.lang.Exception.

java.applet.Applet.showStatus() Show status prints out a message string to the status bar in browser or applet viewer. In this Applet, the URL that will be fetched is displayed in the same Netscape output strip as the URL of a link in generic HTML.

java.awt.MediaTracker Instantiating an object of the class MediaTracker allows you to handle the loading of images gracefully, so that they are not drawn poorly when animations are drawn as they are downloaded. MediaTracker can be used to preload the images and hold them until they are needed.

```
/*
 * Eyecon.java v2.0.1
 * April 7, 1996
 *
 * Copyright (c) 1996 HuskyLabs.
```

```
*
* code by Matthew Ross Davis
* mozart@butterfly.net
*
* interactivity for the masses
*
* Depending on what's given in the tag, this applet will
* show different images and play different sounds
* according to the status of the mouse.
*
* This version is updated from 2.0 to employ showStatus()
* and uses MediaTracker for preloading the images
*
*/

/*here's a sample HTML file tag
<HTML>
<HEAD>
</HEAD>
<BODY>

<applet code="Eyecon.class" width=40 height=40>
<param name="img1" value="images/startup.gif">
<param name="img2" value="images/mouseEnter.gif">
<param name="img3" value="images/mouseDown.gif">
<param name="img4" value="images/mouseUp.gif">
<param name="snd1" value="audio/mouseExit.au">
<param name="snd2" value="audio/mouseEnter.au">
<param name="snd3" value="audio/mouseDown.au">
<param name="snd4" value="audio/mouseUp.au">
<param name="URL" value="http://butterfly.net/mozart/">
</applet>

</BODY>
</HTML>
*/

import java.awt.*;
import java.net.URL;
import java.net.MalformedURLException;
import java.applet.AudioClip;

public class Eyecon extends java.applet.Applet {
```

```java
public String getAppletInfo() {
return "Eyecon - interactive icon applet, by Matthew Ross
  Davis";
}

public String[][] getParameterInfo() {
String[][] info = {
{"img1","image","startup/mouseExit image"},
{"img1","image","mouseEnter image"},
{"img1","image","mouseDown image"},
{"img1","image","mouseUp image"},
{"snd1","sound","mouseExit sound"},
{"snd2","sound","mouseEnter sound"},
{"snd3","sound","mouseDown sound"},
{"snd4","sound","mouseUp sound"},
{"URL","url","linked URL"},
};
return info;
}

// audio objects
AudioClip sound1 = null;
AudioClip sound2 = null;
AudioClip sound3 = null;
AudioClip sound4 = null;

// image objects
Image im1 = null;
Image im2 = null;
Image im3 = null;
Image im4 = null;

// current image for drawing
Image current = null;

// MediaTracker object for loading images
protected MediaTracker trackimgs;

// image and sound filename variables
String imgFile1, imgFile2, imgFile3, imgFile4;
String soundFile1, soundFile2, soundFile3, soundFile4;

// URL variable and object
```

```
String iconURL;
Linkme link;

public void init() {

// assign sound and image filename variables
soundFile1 = getParameter("snd1");
soundFile2 = getParameter("snd2");
soundFile3 = getParameter("snd3");
soundFile4 = getParameter("snd4");
imgFile1 = getParameter("img1");
imgFile2 = getParameter("img2");
imgFile3 = getParameter("img3");
imgFile4 = getParameter("img4");

// the URL and an object to deal with it
iconURL = getParameter("URL");
link = new Linkme(iconURL);

// load the sound files
sound1 = getAudioClip(getCodeBase(), soundFile1);
sound2 = getAudioClip(getCodeBase(), soundFile2);
sound3 = getAudioClip(getCodeBase(), soundFile3);
sound4 = getAudioClip(getCodeBase(), soundFile4);

// create a new MediaTracker object
trackimgs = new MediaTracker(this);

// load the graphics into the objects
// and put each reference into the MediaTracker
im1 = getImage(getCodeBase(), imgFile1);
trackimgs.addImage(im1, 1);
im2 = getImage(getCodeBase(), imgFile2);
trackimgs.addImage(im2, 2);
im3 = getImage(getCodeBase(), imgFile3);
trackimgs.addImage(im3, 3);
im4 = getImage(getCodeBase(), imgFile4);
trackimgs.addImage(im4, 4);

// the following four blocks of code check to see if an
// image exists, then MediaTracker loads the image
if ( im1 != null) {
showStatus("Image 1 is loading");
try { trackimgs.waitForID(1); }
```

```
catch (InterruptedException e) {}
if (trackimgs.isErrorID(1)) {
showStatus("Error with Image 1. Aborting applet.");
return;
}
}

if ( im2 != null ) {
showStatus("Image 2 is loading");
try { trackimgs.waitForID(2); }
catch (InterruptedException e) {}
if (trackimgs.isErrorID(2)) {
showStatus("Error with Image 2. Aborting applet.");
return;
}
}

if ( im3 != null ) {
showStatus("Image 3 is loading");
try { trackimgs.waitForID(3); }
catch (InterruptedException e) {}
if (trackimgs.isErrorID(3)) {
showStatus("Error with Image 3. Aborting applet.");
return;
}
}

if ( im4 != null ) {
showStatus("Image 4 is loading");
try { trackimgs.waitForID(4); }
catch (InterruptedException e) {}
if (trackimgs.isErrorID(4)) {
showStatus("Error with Image 4. Aborting applet.");
return;
}
}

showStatus("Image loading complete. Applet ready.");


// use the mouseEnter() image (im1) on startup
// and resize the applet to image dimensions
if (im1 != null) {
current = im1;
```

```
resize(im1.getWidth(null), im1.getHeight(null));
}
repaint();
}

// on a mouse enter, show the second
// and resize the applet to image dimensions
public boolean mouseEnter(java.awt.Event event, int x,
int y) {
if (im2 != null) {
current = im2;
resize(im2.getWidth(null), im2.getHeight(null));
repaint();
if (sound2 != null)
sound2.play();
}
// show the target URL
showStatus(iconURL);
return true;
}

// on a mouse exit, show the first
// and resize the applet to image dimensions
public boolean mouseExit(java.awt.Event event, int x, int y){
if (im1 != null) {
current = im1;
resize(im1.getWidth(null), im1.getHeight(null));
repaint();
if (sound1 != null)
sound1.play();
}
// clear the target URL
showStatus("");
return true;
}

// on a mouse down, show the third
// and resize the applet to image dimensions
public boolean mouseDown(java.awt.Event event, int x, int y){
if (im3 != null) {
current = im3;
resize(im3.getWidth(null), im3.getHeight(null));
repaint();
if (sound3 != null)
```

```
sound3.play();
}
return true;
}

// on a mouse up, show the fourth
// and resize the applet to image dimensions
 public boolean mouseUp(java.awt.Event event, int x, int y) {
if (im4 != null) {
current = im4;
resize(im4.getWidth(null), im4.getHeight(null));
repaint();
if (sound4 != null)
sound4.play();
}
// link to the URL
getAppletContext().showDocument(link.url);
return true;
}

// draw the current image
public void paint(Graphics g) {
g.drawImage(current, 0, 0, this);
}

// prevent clearing of images - this causes
// the images to be written over each other,
// reducing flicker when they change
public void update(Graphics g) {
paint(g);
}
}


// class for url linking
class Linkme {
URL url;
Linkme(String theURL) {
try { this.url = new URL(theURL); }
catch ( MalformedURLException e) {
System.out.println("Bad URL: " + theURL);
}
```

## CHAPTER 18

Extending an Applet

There are only a few elements that an interface designer wants to have visible on a page. Each designer has a different rule of thumb. Monica recommends no more than five icons on a Web page, if it can be helped. But there is a lot more to get to on a Web site, and it is often frustrating to have to select a link, wait for a download, only to get a second listing of links, click one, and then maybe get sent to a third. By the time you find "content," you're often wondering if it was the right choice, you want to know how many other options there might have been, and you start poking around randomly. With Java, these subcategories can be brought up to the first page and made visible only when the user expresses interest in that category by moving the mouse over a word or icon.

In the Eyecon applet, rather than displaying a second image when the mouse is moved over a graphic, a menu could have dropped with several options for connectivity, rather than just one. Instead of extending that applet any further, we'll take the ImageMap applet that was released with the JDK and construct our own class to extend it. The ImageMap applet was written with extensibility in mind.

Live Feedback ImageMap

When a Java source file is compiled, each class is stored in a separate .class file in the Java bytecode format. If you look in the directory where the ImageMap class is stored, you will see many files with it:

```
http://www.lab.com/LiveJava/developer/imagemap/classes/
index.html
```

Index of livejava/imagemap/classes/index.html

Name	Last modified	Size	Description
Parent Directory			
AniArea.class	23-Apr-96 02:26	1K	
ButtonFilter.class	23-Apr-96 02:27	4K	
ClickArea.class	23-Apr-96 02:27	1K	
DelayedSoundArea.clas+	23-Apr-96 02:27	2K	
HighlightArea.class	23-Apr-96 02:27	1K	
HighlightFilter.class	23-Apr-96 02:27	1K	
HrefButtonArea.class	23-Apr-96 02:27	2K	
ImageMap.class	23-Apr-96 02:27	8K	
ImageMapArea.class	23-Apr-96 02:27	4K	
LinkArea.class	23-Apr-96 02:27	1K	
MenuArea.class	23-Apr-96 02:27	2K	
MenuArea.java	23-Apr-96 02:27	2K	
NameArea.class	23-Apr-96 02:27	1K	
RoundButtonFilter.cla+	23-Apr-96 02:27	2K	
RoundHrefButtonArea.c+	23-Apr-96 02:27	1K	
SoundArea.class	23-Apr-96 02:27	1K	

ImageMap itself does very little more than store an array of ImageMapAreas. ImageMapArea defines a space within ImageMap that will be acted upon when an event occurs there. ImageMap knows that any particular area within it, such as SoundArea, AnimArea and MenuArea, are descended from ImageMapArea and will have certain attributes and behaviors, variables and methods inherited from ImageMapArea. For example, all ImageMapArea descendents will have a getMedia() method, though they will override its implementation in ImageMapArea to get a sound, an animation or whatever the particular descendants need to do their job.

In this example, we created our own class, MenuArea, that is an extension of the work of another programmer, Jim Graham at Sun Microsystems. We happened to have access to the source code, but we could have built on his work without it, by looking at his API documentation and loading his precompiled class files into the same directory as our new class. Theoretically, I could have provided only my new class on the server and loaded the other classes from another host on the network or Internet. Security concerns, however, have led to the implementation in current browsers of a restrictive applet security model that allows the loading of classes only from the host that provided the Web page. Java security will be covered in greater detail in the next section.

Versioning is another issue that emerges in an object-oriented environment, when you base your work on another's classes. If you are dynamically loading objects over a network, and a class has been revised to a new version, your application or applet might break. This happened in a big way when Sun moved from alpha to beta in the Java specifications. The latest version, 1.0, is considered the "frozen API," and later versions are not supposed to make your work unusable. Java Certification through network-based Certificate Authorities and Object Request Brokers (ORBs) are expected to address security and versioning concerns. These will also be covered in greater detail in the next section.

ImageMap Parameters

Let's take a look at our ImageMap example and in particular our MenuArea. Here is the HTML source:

```
</head>
<body>
```

```
<h1>Live Feedback ImageMap</h1>
The image below contains a MenuArea.

<p>

<applet code=ImageMap.class width=300 height=300>
<param name=img value="smiley.jpg">
<param name=highlight value="brighter30">
<param name=area1 value="NameArea,111,80,30,45,That is my
right eye">
<param name=area2 value="HighlightArea,200,200,100,100">
<param name=area3 value="NameArea,170,80,30,35,That is my left
  eye">
<param name=area4 value="MenuArea,100,100,110,50,Links,3">
  <param name=Links,1 value="Sick's homepage,http://www.but-
terfly.net/sick/">
  <param name=Links,2 value="Java homepage,http://www.java
  soft.com">
  <param name=Links,3 value="The Butterfly's Web,http://
www.butterfly.net/">
</applet>

<p>Original artwork &copy; 1996 Michael Reece.
<p>Here is the <a href="MenuArea.java">MenuArea.java</a>
source file.
<hr>
</body>
<address>
<a href="mailto:sick@butterfly.net">sick@butterfly.net</a>
</address>
</html>
```

The parameters of this applet define:

img

the location of the image that is to be displayed, in this case, smiley.jpg.

highlight

how much brighter or darker the highlights should be when an activated area senses a mouse event. This is listed as a percentage brighter or darker than the original image.

startsound
the location of the sound file that is to played when the applet starts.

area
a section of the image that is to be activated by a mouse event.

The Extensible ImageMapArea

As discussed, the ImageMap holds an array of areas. These are rectangles that are passed to the ImageMap applet as:

```
<param name=area[n] value="class, x, y, w, h, arguments>
```

The "class" is the new class that is to be loaded. "X-coordinate," "y-coordinate", "width" and "height" define the rectangular area that the new class has authority over. The "arguments" are specific to new class that is loaded into the applet and executed when an event occurs. ImageMapArea is derived from the basic Object class, since it does not say otherwise. It's a generic space for the ImageMap to act on.

ImageMap instantiates an array of ImageMapAreas. Any subclass of ImageMapArea can fit into that array, allowing different kinds of areas within the map. ImageMapArea is a template that ImageMap knows what to do with. Here are some code samples from ImageMap.

To define a single ImageMapArea, you could do:

```
ImageMapArea area
```

To define an array of areas, you do:

```
ImageMapArea area[]
area[1], area[2], area[i]
```

with i being a loop index variable, meaning that the areas will be processed in order.

```
for (int i = areas.length; --i >= 0; ) {
    areas[i].getMedia();
}
```

The New MenuArea

The new MenuArea that Michael Reece has written to extend Graham's ImageMapArea uses the argument strings to set aside it's own parameters that define the words that will be displayed on pull-down menu and the location of the files to be fetched when a link is selected. So in this example, there is a new type of parameter:

```
<param name=area4 value="MenuArea,100,100,110,50,Links,3">
  <param name=Links,1 value="Sick's homepage,http://www.but-
terfly.net/sick/">
  <param name=Links,2 value="Java homepage,http://www.java-
soft.com">
  <param name=Links,3 value="HuskyLabs,http://www.lab.com/">
```

Where the new area has a value that holds three links, and each link has its own parameter field.

## CHAPTER 19

Classes, Superclasses, Subclasses

Let's capture Graham's ImageMap applet and source code and see what makes it tick. Then we'll look at Michael Reece's MenuArea extension to the basic ImageMap-related classes. You should have the tools to read this code, and from the comments, understand how it operates.

`http://www.lab.com/LiveJava/developers/ImageMap/`

The ImageMap Class

```
/*
 * @(#)ImageMap.java    1.7 96/04/24
 *
 * Copyright (c) 1994-1996 Sun Microsystems, Inc. All Rights
 *    Reserved.
 *
 * Permission to use, copy, modify, and distribute this
 *    software
```

```
import java.applet.Applet;
import java.awt.Image;
```

```
import java.awt.Graphics;
import java.awt.Rectangle;
import java.awt.MediaTracker;
import java.util.StringTokenizer;
import java.util.Vector;
import java.util.Hashtable;
import java.net.URL;
import java.awt.image.ImageProducer;
import java.awt.image.ImageFilter;
import java.awt.image.CropImageFilter;
import java.awt.image.FilteredImageSource;
import java.net.MalformedURLException;

/**
 * An extensible ImageMap applet class.
 * The active areas on the image are controlled by ImageArea
 *   classes
 * that can be dynamically loaded over the net.
 *
 * @author      Jim Graham
 * @version     1.7, 04/24/96
 */
public class ImageMap extends Applet implements Runnable {
    /**
     * The unhighlighted image being mapped.
     */
    Image baseImage;

    /**
     * The list of image area handling objects;
     */
    ImageMapArea areas[];

    /**
     * The primary highlight mode to be used.
     */
    static final int BRIGHTER = 0;
    static final int DARKER = 1;

    int hlmode = BRIGHTER;

    /**
```

```
 * The percentage of highlight to apply for the primary
 *    highlight mode.
 */
int hlpercent = 50;

/**
 * The MediaTracker for loading and constructing the
 *    various images.
 */
MediaTracker tracker;

/**
 * Get a rectangular region of the baseImage highlighted
 *    according to
 * the primary highlight specification.
 */
Image getHighlight(int x, int y, int w, int h) {
    return getHighlight(x, y, w, h, hlmode, hlpercent);
}

/**
 * Get a rectangular region of the baseImage with a
 *    specific highlight.
 */
Image getHighlight(int x, int y, int w, int h, int mode,
  int percent) {
    return getHighlight(x, y, w, h, new
      HighlightFilter(mode == BRIGHTER,percent));
}

/**
 * Get a rectangular region of the baseImage modified by an
 *    image filter.
 */
Image getHighlight(int x, int y, int w, int h, ImageFilter
  filter) {
    ImageFilter cropfilter = new CropImageFilter
      (x, y, w, h);
    ImageProducer prod = new FilteredImageSource
      (baseImage.getSource(),cropfilter);
    return makeImage(prod, filter, 0);
}

/**
 * Make a filtered image based on another image.
```

```
 */
Image makeImage(Image orig, ImageFilter filter) {
    return makeImage(orig.getSource(), filter);
}

/**
 * Make a filtered image based on another ImageProducer.
 */
Image makeImage(ImageProducer prod, ImageFilter filter) {
    return makeImage(prod, filter,
            (prod == baseImage.getSource()) ? 1 : 0);
}

/**
 * Make a filtered image based on another ImageProducer.
 * Add it to the media tracker using the indicated ID.
 */
Image makeImage(ImageProducer prod, ImageFilter filter,
  int ID) {
    Image filtered = createImage(new
      FilteredImageSource(prod, filter));
    tracker.addImage(filtered, ID);
    return filtered;
}

/**
 * Add an image to the list of images to be tracked.
 */
void addImage(Image img) {
    tracker.addImage(img, 1);
}

/**
 * Parse a string representing the desired highlight to be
 *    applied.
 */
void parseHighlight(String s) {
    if (s == null) {
        return;
    }
    if (s.startsWith("brighter")) {
        hlmode = BRIGHTER;
        if (s.length() > "brighter".length()) {
```

```
                    hlpercent = Integer.parseInt(s.sub
                      string("brighter".length()));
            }
        } else if (s.startsWith("darker")) {
            hlmode = DARKER;
            if (s.length() > "darker".length()) {
                hlpercent = Integer.parseInt(
                s.substring("darker".length()));
            }
        }
    }
}

/**
 * Initialize the applet. Get attributes.
 *
 * Initialize the ImageAreas.
 * Each ImageArea is a subclass of the class ImageArea, and
 *    is
 * specified with an attribute of the form:
 *         areaN=ImageAreaClassName,arguments...
 * The ImageAreaClassName is parsed off and a new instance
 *    of that
 * class is created.  The initializer for that class is
 *    passed a
 * reference to the applet and the remainder of the
 *    attribute
 * string, from which the class should retrieve any
 *    information it
 * needs about the area it controls and the actions it
 *    needs to
 * take within that area.
 */
public void init() {
    String s;

    tracker = new MediaTracker(this);
    parseHighlight(getParameter("highlight"));
    introTune = getParameter("startsound");
    baseImage = getImage(getDocumentBase(),
      getParameter("img"));
    Vector areaVec = new Vector();
    int num = 1;
    while (true) {
```

```
ImageMapArea newArea;
s = getParameter("area"+num);
if (s == null) {
    // Try rect for backwards compatibility.
    s = getParameter("rect"+num);
    if (s == null) {
        break;
    }
    try {
        newArea = new HighlightArea();
        newArea.init(this, s);
        areaVec.addElement(newArea);
        String url = getParameter("href"+num);
        if (url != null) {
            s += "," + url;
            newArea = new LinkArea();
            newArea.init(this, s);
            areaVec.addElement(newArea);
        }
    } catch (Exception e) {
      System.out.println("error processing: "+s);
        e.printStackTrace();
        break;
    }
} else {
    try {
        int classend = s.indexOf(",");
        String name = s.substring(0, classend);
        newArea = (ImageMapArea) Class.
          forName(name).newInstance();
        s = s.substring(classend+1);
        newArea.init(this, s);
        areaVec.addElement(newArea);
    } catch (Exception e) {
      System.out.println("error processing: "+s);
        e.printStackTrace();
        break;
    }
}
num++;
}
areas = new ImageMapArea[areaVec.size()];
areaVec.copyInto(areas);
```

```
            checkSize();
        }

    Thread aniThread = null;
    String introTune = null;

    public void start() {
        if (introTune != null)
            try {
                play(new URL(getDocumentBase(), introTune));
            }
    catch (MalformedURLException e) {}
        if (aniThread == null) {
            aniThread = new Thread(this);
            aniThread.setName("ImageMap Animator");
            aniThread.start();
        }
    }

    public void run() {
        Thread me = Thread.currentThread();
        tracker.checkAll(true);
        for (int i = areas.length; --i >= 0; ) {
            areas[i].getMedia();
        }
        me.setPriority(Thread.MIN_PRIORITY);
        while (aniThread == me) {
            boolean animating = false;
            for (int i = areas.length; --i >= 0; ) {
                animating = areas[i].animate() || animating;
            }
            try {
                synchronized(this) {
                    wait(animating ? 100 : 0);
                }
            }
    catch (InterruptedException e) {
                break;
            }
        }
    }

    public synchronized void startAnimation() {
```

```
        notify();
    }

    public synchronized void stop() {
        aniThread = null;
        notify();
        for (int i = 0; i < areas.length; i++) {
            areas[i].exit();
        }
    }

    /**
     * Check the size of this applet while the image is being
     *     loaded.
     */
    void checkSize() {
        int w = baseImage.getWidth(this);
        int h = baseImage.getHeight(this);
        if (w > 0 && h > 0) {
            resize(w, h);
            synchronized(this) {
                fullrepaint = true;
            }
            repaint(0, 0, w, h);
        }
    }

    private boolean fullrepaint = false;
    private final static long UPDATERATE = 100;

    /**
     * Handle updates from images being loaded.
     */
    public boolean imageUpdate(Image img, int infoflags,
        int x, int y, int width, int
        height) {
        if ((infoflags & (WIDTH | HEIGHT)) != 0) {
            checkSize();
        }
        if ((infoflags & (SOMEBITS | FRAMEBITS | ALLBITS))
        != 0) {
        synchronized(this) {
```

```
                        fullrepaint = true;
            }
            repaint((((infoflags & (FRAMEBITS | ALLBITS)) != 0)
            ? 0 : UPDATERATE,
            x, y, width, height);
        }
        return (infoflags & (ALLBITS | ERROR)) == 0;
    }

    /**
     * Paint the image and all active highlights.
     */
    public void paint(Graphics g) {
        synchronized(this) {
            fullrepaint = false;
        }
        if (baseImage == null) {
            return;
        }
        g.drawImage(baseImage, 0, 0, this);
        if (areas != null) {
            for (int i = areas.length; --i >= 0; ) {
                areas[i].highlight(g);
            }
        }
    }

    /**
     * Update the active highlights on the image.
     */
    public void update(Graphics g) {
        boolean full;
        synchronized(this) {
            full = fullrepaint;
        }
        if (full) {
            paint(g);
            return;
        }
        if (baseImage == null) {
            return;
        }
        g.drawImage(baseImage, 0, 0, this);
```

```
        if (areas == null) {
            return;
        }
        // First unhighlight all of the deactivated areas
        for (int i = areas.length; --i >= 0; ) {
            areas[i].highlight(g);
        }
    }

    /**
     * Make sure that no ImageAreas are highlighted.
     */
    public boolean mouseExit(java.awt.Event evt, int x, int y)
{
        for (int i = 0; i < areas.length; i++) {
            areas[i].checkExit();
        }

        return true;
    }

    /**
     * Find the ImageAreas that the mouse is in.
     */
    public boolean mouseMove(java.awt.Event evt, int x, int y)
{
        boolean eaten = false;

        for (int i = 0; i < areas.length; i++) {
            if (!eaten && areas[i].inside(x, y)) {
                eaten = areas[i].checkEnter(x, y);
            } else {
                areas[i].checkExit();
            }
        }

        return true;
    }

    int pressX;
    int pressY;

    /**
```

```
 * Inform all active ImageAreas of a mouse press.
 */
public boolean mouseDown(java.awt.Event evt, int x, int y)
  {
      pressX = x;
      pressY = y;

      for (int i = 0; i < areas.length; i++) {
          if (areas[i].inside(x, y)) {
              if (areas[i].press(x, y)) {
                  break;
              }
          }
      }

      return true;
  }

/**
 * Inform all active ImageAreas of a mouse release.
 * Only those areas that were inside the original
 *    mouseDown()
 * are informed of the mouseUp.
 */
public boolean mouseUp(java.awt.Event evt, int x, int y) {
      for (int i = 0; i < areas.length; i++) {
          if (areas[i].inside(pressX, pressY)) {
              if (areas[i].lift(x, y)) {
                  break;
              }
          }
      }

      return true;
  }

/**
 * Inform all active ImageAreas of a mouse drag.
 * Only those areas that were inside the original
 *    mouseDown()
 * are informed of the mouseUp.
 */
```

```
public boolean mouseDrag(java.awt.Event evt, int x, int y)
 {
    mouseMove(evt, x, y);
    for (int i = 0; i < areas.length; i++) {
        if (areas[i].inside(pressX, pressY)) {
            if (areas[i].drag(x, y)) {
                break;
            }
        }
    }

    return true;
}

/**
 * Scan all areas looking for the topmost status string.
 */
public void newStatus() {
    String msg = null;
    for (int i = 0; i < areas.length; i++) {
        msg = areas[i].getStatus(msg);
    }
    showStatus(msg);
}
```

The ImageMapArea Superclass

```
/*
 * @(#)ImageMapArea.java        1.5 96/04/24
 *
 * Copyright (c) 1994-1996 Sun Microsystems, Inc. All Rights
 *    Reserved.
 *
 * Permission to use, copy, modify, and distribute this
 *    software
 * and its documentation for NON-COMMERCIAL or COMMERCIAL
 *    purposes and
 * without fee is hereby granted.
 * Please refer to the file http://java.sun.com/
 * copy_trademarks.html
```

```
 * for further important copyright and trademark information
 *    and to
 * http://java.sun.com/licensing.html for further important
 *    licensing
 * information for the Java (tm) Technology.
 *
 * SUN MAKES NO REPRESENTATIONS OR WARRANTIES ABOUT THE
 *    SUITABILITY OF
 * THE SOFTWARE, EITHER EXPRESS OR IMPLIED, INCLUDING BUT NOT
 *    LIMITED
 * TO THE IMPLIED WARRANTIES OF MERCHANTABILITY, FITNESS FOR A
 * PARTICULAR PURPOSE, OR NON-INFRINGEMENT. SUN SHALL NOT BE
 *    LIABLE FOR
 * ANY DAMAGES SUFFERED BY LICENSEE AS A RESULT OF USING,
 *    MODIFYING OR
 * DISTRIBUTING THIS SOFTWARE OR ITS DERIVATIVES.
 *
 * THIS SOFTWARE IS NOT DESIGNED OR INTENDED FOR USE OR RESALE
 *    AS ON-LINE
 * CONTROL EQUIPMENT IN HAZARDOUS ENVIRONMENTS REQUIRING
 *    FAIL-SAFE
 * PERFORMANCE, SUCH AS IN THE OPERATION OF NUCLEAR
 *    FACILITIES, AIRCRAFT
 * NAVIGATION OR COMMUNICATION SYSTEMS, AIR TRAFFIC CONTROL,
 *    DIRECT LIFE
 * SUPPORT MACHINES, OR WEAPONS SYSTEMS, IN WHICH THE FAILURE
 *    OF THE
 * SOFTWARE COULD LEAD DIRECTLY TO DEATH, PERSONAL INJURY, OR
 *    SEVERE
 * PHYSICAL OR ENVIRONMENTAL DAMAGE ("HIGH RISK
 *    ACTIVITIES").   SUN
 * SPECIFICALLY DISCLAIMS ANY EXPRESS OR IMPLIED WARRANTY OF
 *    FITNESS FOR
 * HIGH RISK ACTIVITIES.
 */

import java.awt.Graphics;
import java.awt.Image;
import java.awt.image.*;
import java.util.StringTokenizer;
import java.net.URL;
import java.net.MalformedURLException;
```

```
/**
 * The base ImageArea class.
 * This class performs the basic functions that most ImageArea
 * classes will need and delegates specific actions to the
 *   subclasses.
 *
 * @author    Jim Graham
 * @version   1.5, 04/24/96
 */
class ImageMapArea implements ImageObserver {
    /** The applet parent that contains this ImageArea. */
    ImageMap parent;
    /** The X location of the area (if rectangular). */
    int X;
    /** The Y location of the area (if rectangular). */
    int Y;
    /** The size().width of the area (if rectangular). */
    int W;
    /** The size().height of the area (if rectangular). */
    int H;
    /**
     * This flag indicates whether the user was in this area
     *   during the
     * last scan of mouse locations.
     */
    boolean entered = false;
    /** This flag indicates whether the area is currently
     *   highlighted.
     */
    boolean active = false;

    /**
     * This is the default highlight image if no special
     *   effects are
     * needed to draw the highlighted image.  It is created by
     *   the
     * default "makeImages()" method.
     */
    Image hlImage;

    /**
     * This is the status string requested by this area. Only
```

```
    * the status string from the topmost area which has
      requested one
    * will be displayed.
    */
   String status;

   /**
    * Initialize this ImageArea as called from the applet.
    * If the subclass does not override this initializer, then
    *    it
    * will perform the basic functions of setting the parent
    *    applet
    * and parsing out 4 numbers from the argument string which
    *    specify
    * a rectangular region for the ImageArea to act on.
    * The remainder of the argument string is passed to the
    *    handleArg()
    * method for more specific handling by the subclass.
    */
   public void init(ImageMap parent, String args) {
       this.parent = parent;
       StringTokenizer st = new StringTokenizer(args, ", ");
       X = Integer.parseInt(st.nextToken());
       Y = Integer.parseInt(st.nextToken());
       W = Integer.parseInt(st.nextToken());
       H = Integer.parseInt(st.nextToken());
       if (st.hasMoreTokens()) {
           // hasMoreTokens() Skips the trailing comma
           handleArg(st.nextToken(""));
       } else {
           handleArg(null);
       }
       makeImages();
   }

   /**
    * This method handles the remainder of the argument string
    *    after
    * the standard initializer has parsed off the 4
    *    rectangular
    * parameters.  If the subclass does not override this
    *    method,
    * the remainder will be ignored.
    */
   public void handleArg(String s) {
```

```
}

/**
 * This method loads any additional media that the
 *    ImageMapArea
 * may need for its animations.
 */
public void getMedia() {
}

/**
 * This method is called every animation cycle if there are
 *    any
 * active animating areas.
 * @return true if this area requires further animation
     notifications
 */
public boolean animate() {
    return false;
}

/**
 * This method sets the image to be used to render the
 *    ImageArea
 * when it is highlighted.
 */
public void setHighlight(Image img) {
    hlImage = img;
}

/**
 * This method handles the construction of the various
 *    images
 * used to highlight this particular ImageArea when the
 *    user
 * interacts with it.
 */
public void makeImages() {
    setHighlight(parent.getHighlight(X, Y, W, H));
}

/**
```

```
 * The repaint method causes the area to be repainted at
 *    the next
 * opportunity.
 */
public void repaint() {
    parent.repaint(0, X, Y, W, H);
}


/**
 * This method tests to see if a point is inside this
 * ImageArea.
 * The standard method assumes a rectangular area as
 * parsed by
 * the standard initializer.  If a more complex area is
 * required
 * then this method will have to be overridden by the sub
 * class.
 */
public boolean inside(int x, int y) {
    return (x >= X && x < (X + W) && y >= Y && y < (Y + H));
}


/**
 * This utility method draws a rectangular subset of a
 *    highlight
 * image.
 */
public void drawImage(Graphics g, Image img, int imgx, int
  imgy,int x, int y, int w, int h) {
    Graphics ng = g.create();
    ng.clipRect(x, y, w, h);
    ng.drawImage(img, imgx, imgy, this);
}


/**
 * This method handles the updates from drawing the
 * images.
 */
public boolean imageUpdate(Image img, int infoflags,
    int x, int y, int width, int height) {
    if (img == hlImage) {
        return parent.imageUpdate(img, infoflags,
```

```
            x + X, y + Y,width, height);
        } else {
            return (infoflags & (ALLBITS | ERROR)) == 0;
        }
    }

/**
 * This utility method records a string to be shown in the
 *    status bar.
 */
public void showStatus(String msg) {
    status = msg;
    parent.newStatus();
}

/**
 * This utility method returns the status string this area
 *    wants to
 * put into the status bar.  If no previous area (higher in
 *    the
 * stacking order) has yet returned a status message, pre
 *    vmsg will
 * be null and this area will then return its own message,
 *    otherwise
 * it will leave the present message alone.
 */
public String getStatus(String prevmsg) {
    return (prevmsg == null) ? status : prevmsg;
}

/**
 * This utility method tells the browser to visit a URL.
 */
public void showDocument(URL u) {
    parent.getAppletContext().showDocument(u);
}

/**
 * This method highlights the specified area when the user
 *    enters
 * it with his mouse.  The standard highlight method is to
 *    replace
```

```
 * the indicated rectangular area of the image with the
 *   primary
 * highlighted image.
 */
public void highlight(Graphics g) {
}

/**
 * The checkEnter method is called when the mouse is inside
 *   the
 * region to see if the area needs to have its enter method
 *   called.
 * The default implementation simply checks if the entered
 *   flag is
 * set and only calls enter if it is false.
 */
public boolean checkEnter(int x, int y) {
    if (!entered) {
        entered = true;
        enter(x, y);
    }
    return isTerminal();
}

/**
 * The checkExit method is called when the mouse is outside
 *   the
 * region to see if the area needs to have its exit method
 *   called.
 * The default implementation simply checks if the entered
 *   flag is
 * set and only calls exit if it is true.
 */
public void checkExit() {
    if (entered) {
        entered = false;
        exit();
    }
}

/**
```

```
 * The isTerminal method controls whether events propagate
 *   to the
 * areas which lie beneath this one.
 * @return true if the events should be propagated to the
 *   underlying
 * areas.
 */
public boolean isTerminal() {
    return false;
}

/**
 * The enter method is called when the mouse enters the
 *   region.
 * The location is supplied, but the standard
 *   implementation is
 * to call the overloaded method with no arguments.
 */
public void enter(int x, int y) {
    enter();
}

/**
 * The overloaded enter method is called when the mouse
 *   enters
 * the region.  This method can be overridden if the
 *   ImageArea
 * does not need to know where the mouse entered.
 */
public void enter() {
}

/**
 * The exit method is called when the mouse leaves the
 *   region.
 */
public void exit() {
}

/**
 * The press method is called when the user presses the
 *   mouse
```

```
 * button inside the ImageArea.  The location is supplied,
 *    but
 * the standard implementation is to call the overloaded
 *    method
 * with no arguments.
 * @return true if this ImageMapArea wants to prevent any
 *    underlying
 * areas from seeing the press
 */
public boolean press(int x, int y) {
    return press();
}

/**
 * The overloaded press method is called when the user
 *    presses the
 * mouse button inside the ImageArea.  This method can be
 *    overridden
 * if the ImageArea does not need to know the location of
 *    the press.
 * @return true if this ImageMapArea wants to prevent any
 *    underlying
 * areas from seeing the press
 */
public boolean press() {
    return isTerminal();
}

/**
 * The lift method is called when the user releases the
 *    mouse button.
 * The location is supplied, but the standard
 *    implementation is to
 * call the overloaded method with no arguments.  Only
 *    those ImageAreas
 * that were informed of a press will be informed of the
 *    corresponding
 * release.
 * @return true if this ImageMapArea wants to prevent any
 *    underlying
 * areas from seeing the lift
 */
```

```
public boolean lift(int x, int y) {
    return lift();
}

/**
 * The overloaded lift method is called when the user
 *   releases the
 * mouse button.  This method can be overridden if the
 *   ImageArea
 * does not need to know the location of the release.
 * @return true if this ImageMapArea wants to prevent any
 *   underlying
 * areas from seeing the lift
 */
public boolean lift() {
    return isTerminal();
}

/**
 * The drag method is called when the user moves the mouse
 *   while
 * the button is pressed.  Only those ImageAreas that were
 *   informed
 * of a press will be informed of the corresponding mouse
 *   movements.
 * @return true if this ImageMapArea wants to prevent any
 *   underlying
 * areas from seeing the drag
 */
public boolean drag(int x, int y)
return isTerminal();
```

The MenuArea Subclass

```
/*
 * @(#)MenuArea.java    1.0 04/22/96    sick@butterfly.net
 *
 * Copyright (c) 1996 HuskyLabs, Inc. All rights reserved.
 *
 */
```

```
import java.awt.Color;
import java.awt.Graphics;
import java.net.URL;
import java.net.MalformedURLExcepion;
/**
 * A pop-up menu ImageArea class.
 * This class extends the basic ImageMapArea Class to show a
 *   pop-up menu when
 * the mouse enters the area.
 *
 * @author  Michael Reece <sick@butterfly.net>
 * @version 1.0 04/22/96
 */
class MenuArea extends ImageMapArea {

    String[] items = null;   // menu item names
    String[] links = null;   // menu item links
    int len = 0;             // number of items

    boolean visible = false;    // is menu visible?


    /**
     * The argument string is the menu name and length.
     * (ie, menu1,4)
     */
    public void handleArg(String arg) {
        // parse name and length
        int i = arg.indexOf(',');
        String name = arg.substring(0,i);
        len = Integer.parseInt(arg.substring(i+1));

        // set up arrays
        items = new String[len];
        links = new String[len];

        // get each menu item "name,i"
        for (i = 1; i <= len; i++) {
            String s = parent.getParameter(name + "," + i);
            // parse item name and link
            int j = s.indexOf(',');
            String n = s.substring(0,j);
```

```
        String l = s.substring(j+1);
        // place in array
        items[i-1] = n;
        links[i-1] = l;
    }
}


/**
 * "hilight" the area by showing the menu, if visible
 */
public void highlight(Graphics g) {
    if (visible) {
        g.setColor(Color.lightGray);
        g.fill3DRect(X, Y, W, H, true);
        g.setColor(Color.black);
        for (int i = 1; i <= len; i++) {
            // draw each item, 5 pixel over, 15 pixels down
            //   for each
            g.drawString(items[i-1], X+5, Y+(i*15));
        }
    }
}


/**
 * the mouse has entered the area, set visible to true
 */
public boolean enter() {
    visible = true;
    repaint();
    return true;
}


/**
 * the mouse has left, set visible to false
 */
public void exit() {
    visible = false;
    repaint();
}
```

```
/**
 * a mouse press, go to the link
 */
public boolean lift(int x, int y) {
    if (inside(x, y)) {
        // get index, by determining mouse offset from Y
        //    and di3viding by 15
        int i = (y-Y) / 15;
        if (i >= len) {
            // just in case the menu is extra long
            showStatus("no item there");
            return false;
        }
        // show the document
        try {
          URL url = new URL(links[i]);
          showDocument(url);
        } catch (MalformedURLException e) {
            showStatus("bad link " + links[i]);
        }
        return true;
    }
    return false;
}

} // class MenuArea
```

III. Tactical Java

From harbaugh@acusys.com Thu Jun 20 18:03:10 1996
Date: Thu, 23 May 1996 20:48:47 +0600
From: "Sam Harbaugh (AQ)" <harbaugh@acusys.com>
To: David Levine <motodave@butterfly.net>
Subject: Harbaugh's Reset Button Story

Dr. Sam Harbaugh's Reset Button Story

Future anthropologists will note the passing of the computer reset button to be as significant in man's evolution as man first walking erect. The lack of a reset button will signal that software at last has full control of the hardware. The passing of the reset button will allow mankind to proliferate computers in unattended situations and will cause a knee in the computer population growth curve.

Let us designate the time of this passing as K=0. Previous time will be termed BK (before komputers) and time after termed AK (after komputers).

Future anthropologists will note the following:

In BK it was necessary to lay hands on a rogue computer to regain control. The hardware was controlled by an incredibly complex piece of software called an operating system (OS).

The operating system would often get confused. Even worse it would turn control of the hardware over to application software which was even more likely to misbehave. In either case it would require that a person push keys and buttons to restore operation. A person would try key combinations and if those failed, push the reset button. Sometimes a person would have to unpower and repower the hardware to restore operation. This behavior limited the usage of computers to non-critical applications and to places where people were available.

Researchers studying the usage of inter-machine communications may designate I=0 as the time when the number of
internet connections equalled the number of people. They
may reason that K=0 was very close to I=0 because the
unattended computers accounted for the largest number of
internet connections.

In a down-to-earth, present day technology situation the
realization would be a Java machine interpreting byte
code where the Java machine has complete control of the
hardware and never turns control over to the application.

Asides: I attended a trade show where an IBM person
(almost as old as me) stood proudly at a large photo of
a PowerPC chip. I asked "will the PowerPC have a reset
button?". He said "yes, of course". I told the above
story about the need for software to have complete control over the hardware. He looked into space and said
"You know, that's the way it used to be".

sam harbaugh harbaugh@acusys.com

## CHAPTER 20

The Applet and the Enterprise

The Corporate Intranet

Act I. In which the consultant observes corporate culture.

Once up on a time, a well-groomed consultant arrived at Corpus, a mega-multi-national corporation, looking not to revolutionize the way they do business, but just for some work on an hourly basis. He arrived a few hours before his appointment, hoping to chat with some of the technical staff before meeting with the executives, but they were busy integrating new systems, applications and networks and extending their product, distribution and inventory databases to handle the new requirements continually being passed down to IS from above.

Each database redesign requires modifications of front end (developed using Visual Basic for the PC) as Windows dominates the desktops internally and among trusted third parties, such as distributors, major corporate customers, suppliers/manufacturers and advertising agencies who need to query the database and input information through remote-access dial-up connections, over a virtual private (Frame-Relay) network and through the Internet (proxied at a firewall, authenticated with public and private keys, and encrypted through an SSL layer).

The marketing department are on Macintoshes, so they don't have direct access to the corporate data, but that doesn't really matter. They run FileMaker Pro and 4D to keep track of what they're spending with the ad agencies, on direct mail and in creative services. They had gone ahead and hired a 4D/Mac guy to build their databases, and can pretty much maintain them on their own, with his occasional support. Except now they want to be able to perform relational queries against the sales records to analyze the impact of new targeted campaigns.

The sales group is still mostly on dumb terminals connected to a VAX cluster, which is for the best. They have all the SKU numbers, customer codes, and inventory at their fingertips. They can see when products are shipped and by what transportation method, so they can answer customer queries. The warehouse also runs on VAX, so when orders are logged, data is also in the fulfillment system. Some of the sales managers, who also need to do a lot of word processing and use spreadsheets, have PCs, but most of their work is done through terminal emulation to the VAX. The VAX cluster runs the central, mission-critical systems at Corpus.

The sales folk don't need much in the way of technical knowledge of the products, as they take orders directly from SKUs supplied by the customers, who all have a big catalog on their desks. When there is a technical question, the sales people transfer the call to the technical sales and support center. The technical support group has an extensive product database with figures and diagrams and manuals for over 150,000 products. They pull this off a multiprocessing UNIX box running Informix with custom 4GL code. A Windows-based Power-Builder front-end is about to be deployed.

The nifty thing is that the big customer catalog is developed off this same database using SGML and FrameMaker. Customer catalogs can be printed from relational queries on the database, marked up on the fly, and sent to a postscript printer.

The consultant was good. He gleaned all this from folders carried by staff he passed in the hall, snippets of conversation at the coffeepot, and a glance through the glass of the computer center and the books lining the upper shelves of the cubicles he passed while being escorted from the reception area back to the executive conference room. He knew why he had been called. The systems were mostly very advanced, the work environment seemed good. The technical staff was tan, which was a sure sign that the systems and network were fairly stable. And these were not monitor tans. But the first symptoms of an infection were showing, and unless checked would result in the "naturally evolving" rather than the "Architechted" Intranet. In the naturally evolving architecture, small user groups have become frustrated with the monolithic corporate information infrastructure and begin to keep their own databases on pocket LANs. This is seldom keyed to the central records. They develop their own business logic and interfaces. They are successful, to a degree, but lose the ability to share their knowledge.

They were migrating towards an Intranet architecture, which leverages Internet technologies and standards to assure interoperability. In each instance he saw where Java could solve a problem.

The consultant entered a conference room. He was offered coffee and seated at an expansive oval oak table. The chairs had armrests. He was served coffee in a porcelain cup from a great silver urn. He drank his coffee with cream, and was offered more. An hour later, five people entered the room. They were introduced as the CEO, the CIO, the CFO, the CTO and the COO. They got right down to business.

Strategic Development

Act II. In which the consultant is briefed on Corpus strategic initiatives.

A CAD (computer-aided design) program was in late beta and about to be shipped to retailers that would display acceptable merchandise placement in consumer outlets. Originally, the application was going to dial into a modem bank and download the latest approved designs, which could be manipulated in the application, products stacked and unstacked, placed in an environment of other goods, aisles and exits, and coordinates plotted. With the growth of the Internet, and ready availability of regional connectivity, it was decided that a private retailer's web would be established, and retailers would be instructed to set a MIME-type on their browser that would cause the custom CAD program to launch upon transfer of the CAD file. Now with plug-ins, the application developers are considering not shipping the full CAD application at all, and letting it launch on the desktop, but providing a Netscape plug-in that would allow the manipulation of the CAD file within the context of the browser. The consultant saw a good opportunity to use Java Beans and other cross-API interoperability suites to distribute the CAD viewer with the data.

Mailing lists and bulletin boards were being moved from proprietary dial-up applications, such as First Class, to Internet-based applications, such as majordomo, HyperMail, and INN (Usenet-style) internal newsgroups. The consultant saw the move toward interoperable, open systems as a good sign. TCP/IP client software suites were plentiful, and would soon be available in Java packages, even pre-bundled with Network Computers.

A large Lotus Notes initiative that had been on the verge of approval was put on hold. He understood this was due to competition from Intranet-based solutions from Netscape. While Lotus Notes was agressively incorporating Java, Hot Java and Netscape's server suite make Lotus Notes essentially obsolete.

Another consultant was advising them to abandon their very costly third-party remote access database projects, currently under development in Visual Basic on other client/server Rapid Application Development environments, in favor of using Netscape with Oracle/

OraPERL or Procedural SQL or Sybase/SybPERL on the server/CGI side. Database queries would be done through HTML forms, and the results would be displayed in HTML generated on the fly through PERL scripts or stored procedures. The PL/SQL would perform better but would take longer to develop and be more difficult to modify. What about CORBA (Common Object Request Broker Architecture)? Is it ready for prime time? Java front-ends would be able to maintain "state," continuous sessions with the database server, while HTTP would need to send back a completely new screen after each query.

The reason for moving from Visual Basic to an Intranet solution was that the client applications that were being developed were becoming very bloated and that all the different users would need only a small subset of the capabilities. Each user could have a different Web-page interface. They would learn that this was even more natural for Java. It did not make much sense to distribute the whole application to all the different types of database customers, but it also did not make sense to develop custom applications for each group. There were also data security and integrity issues, as certain sales data could not be made available to competing distributors or retailers. On the network security side, maintaining large modem banks that connected directly to the network was a procedural nightmare. By moving to a Web-based query system, all queries could come through a proxy-based firewall that proxied SSL and other encryption schemes, without building an IP transport stack and SSL into the custom Windows software, which used WinCLI (Windows Call Level Interface) as the transport layer. Using server-push in the CGI when a user first logs into the site, the user would see only the interface, environment and forms related to data that was permissible to access. The main drawback was that socket connections could not be kept open, so very large solution sets needed to be sent enmasse across the network. The user interface was also limited to the capabilities of HTML extensions.

Management, Scalability, and Extensibility

ACT III. The Issue. In which the consultant understands the Corpus pain.

So what was the problem? What is the straw that is beginning to weigh heavily on this camel's back? It seemed like a small one. Consumers.

Corpus has begun a direct sales channel under a new name for its own products and even those of some of its manufacturing competitors. There was a high-level initiative under way to reposition the company with consumers, to develop brand recognition, rather than relying on wholesalers, retailers and complex distribution channels. A small piece of this had been the establishment on the Internet of a Web site with the entire product line. This was done fairly gingerly, with listings of regional resellers and wholesalers, and limited consumer ordering capability, so as not to disturb their distributors. However, the executives were ready to admit that the ultimate goal was to cut out the middleman and ultimately sell directly to the consumer.

The pain came in with the sales and support groups, who were accustomed to working with business customers. All of a sudden, people were coming on the line who didn't know what product they were using, what model, brand, or year. Some had lost the instructions or the product itself and couldn't give a clear enough description to enable the sales rep to help them. The customer databases were not yet set up to relate product purchase history to individual consumers, so the salesperson had no way to know what product was bought. This also limited upselling, as the sales rep could not tell what component might fit in with the over product configuration owned by the consumer. On products that were manufactured by other companies, but sold through the new sales group, a customer database would have to be built from scratch, unless a backdoor gateway between the two companies could be established.

The obvious solution was to give the sales reps a browser and access to the same product information that the consumer had on the Web. At least the salespeople would have the graphics at their fingertips and could navigate through searches and hypertext links through the information. If the sales rep was lucky enough to have a customer with a Web connection, the two could view the same database, and determine the exact product in question. The major drawback, though, was that the sales people did not have PCs. They were on terminals. Adding that many PCs on the network would cost a significant chunk of change, plus support costs and software. An experienced sales rep could navigate through a database much more rapidly with both hands on the keyboard than by clicking through with a mouse.

Of course, every consultant came in with an agenda: move them to NT, add PCs, decentralize, add an ODBC layer and connect disparate databases over the network, webify, Intranets, public and private key encryption, certificate authorities, firewalls, centralize, move to DEC Alphas, middleware, networked multimedia, shared whiteboards... There seemed to be a lot of little patches but no real solution.

Auditing and Evaluating the Enterprise

Act IV. The Chalk Talk. In which the consultant takes the stage.

The consultant nodded gravely through the various presentations.

He walked up to the whiteboard, picked up a marker, and summarized what he'd heard. He drew out the various networks. He listed the applications and protocols, the systems and gateways. He drew up a list of goals and objectives. He solicited feedback from the executives, trying to quantify the in-house skills and resources. He recreated the history of organization's computing infrastructure from its earliest days to the present. When he was done, he had something like this:

```
http://www.lab.com/LiveJava/developers/intranet.html
```

The executives nodded. That was indeed the situation, accurately represented. In the process of reiterating, they had filled in even more requirements, such as interoperation with EDI systems that some of their government customers were using and an interface to Human Resources, to track employee productivity, and accounting.

So, said the CEO, what's your recommendation?

Approaching a Systems Redesign: Think Small

Act V. In which the consultant makes his recommendation.

The consultant considered the options. He knew what needed to be done but didn't know how to present it. The solution had to be simple, elegant, yet provide a vast array of capabilities. Finally he spoke.

"One button," he said.

"That's what you need. *One button.*"

"We need to view this from the user's perspective, and every user is different. They have different needs, different roles, different responsibilities, different levels of access. We also need to view this from the management side, how these users can be supported and how the systems can be protected. One thing is clear, though, and that is that the answer does not lie on the desktop, or on the server, or on the network. The answer does not lie in the database, or in the applications. It lies in the role of the user, the user's need for information, the user's ability to add to the store of knowledge, and most important, the user's need to communicate with coworker, customer, partner or vendor.

"As we know, computers are no longer for calculating but for communicating and, in particular, providing the framework for informed communications. The answer to our systems questions lies the user's relationship with the enterprise. When the users boot up the machine, or turn on the monitor or launch an application, what are they doing? If they are employees, they're going to work. Even if they're in their cubicle already, they're going to work. Customers, what are they doing when they hit your Web site? They're visiting Corpus. And your Web site is saying "Welcome to Corpus." Over the Network, you're visiting your vendors and getting data to match the goods. You view the vendor from your perspective. When the vendor enters your data, it is from a different perspective. As we try to put our arms around it, the issue grows complicated again. So let's stick to our solution: one button.

"We need on each user's desktop a single button. What will that button be labeled? What will that button look like? Will it be an icon or a GUI widget? We'll defer those questions. For now, we will view that button as an Object.

```
Button button
```

"It is an instantiation of the Button class that is part of Java's Abstract Window Toolkit...

"Hold on a minute, son!" said the CIO. "We didn't ask you to come in here and talk to us about Java. We've had Java consultants and developers present, and we have not approved or authorized the use of Java within this institution. We have been reading grave warnings on potential hostile applets and Java attacks from behind the firewall. We will not accept Java until the security issues and performance issues are cleared up."

Java Security and Performance

Act VI. In which the Consultant addresses Java Security.

The consultant was unfazed. "Then let's address those issues now, so we can continue the conversation. Java cannot be ignored. It will not go away, and it is a very useful tool, so we need to determine exactly where it can and should be used, where its use would be inadvisable, and what our alternatives look like.

"The most important thing to understand is that Java addresses the issue of security in its most basic design, as it was designed to inhabit heterogeneous, interconnected network environments. This is not true of other programming languages. The reported security holes that you are referring to are related to the current *implementation* of Java in some commercial products, rather than design flaws. This is not meant to suggest that security concerns are unwarranted, but that Java is an important part of a complete security regimen.

"Built into the Java language are safety rules. As you know, Java byte-codes are interpreted at runtime, when they are recompiled as plat-form-specific instructions. On this client computer, a bytecode verifier is responsible for making sure that the Java language safety rules are implemented correctly and that the creator of the code did not attempt any hostile behavior. This is akin to built-in virus protection.

"Many viruses are created in other programming languages by forging 'pointers.' Pointers are used in nonhostile applications by a program-mer to allocate memory on the computer that runs the software. A hostile programmer could take an integer within the program or a memory cell and use it to address areas of the memory where basic operations are performed, resulting in system errors, application crashes and other malfunctions.

"Java has a completely different means of managing memory, which is not under the control of the programmer and is not implemented by the compiler. All memory allocation and layout decisions are made on the client computer by a run-time system. The Java interpreter will allocate memory differently on different hardware and software plat-forms by resolving symbolic handles to real memory addresses at run time. This is a great aid to the programmer, who does not have to explicitly request memory from the system for application tasks, but it does affect performance. We'll discuss those issues shortly.

"The threat to the casual browser is the hostile applet that performs a *denial of service* attack, meaning that it will try to overwhelm your computer with requests for memory or try to download useless amounts of data, making your computer unable to perform. This attack will probably be averted by restarting the browser. While inconvenient, it poses no real danger. There is also hostile HTML on the Internet, as well as poorly written programs that will have similar adverse effects.

"As far as security is concerned, this approach to memory management does not mean that hostile or annoying Java programs cannot be written intentionally or accidentally or that buggy implementation of the Java Virtual Machine specification will not leave openings for hostile programmers to exploit. It means that the job of the system administrator and network manager becomes much easier when he understands Java's approach to security and can take appropriate measures to maintain the integrity of the systems and network. A good system administrator's concerns with security do not just involve keeping out hackers but incorporate procedures and precautions for a disaster recovery plan. Some of the Sysadmin's tools include:

- A firewall
- Packet filtering on the router
- RAID (Redundant Array of Inexpensive Disks)
- Tape backups (full weekly and incremental daily)
- Virus scanning

"No system is fail-safe, and most damage is caused by user error or employee vengence. Often, hackers become bogeymen who distract a corporation from adequately protecting systems from other threats. Desktop computers running a version of Windows or the MacOS generally require thousands of dollars of maintenance a year, as users delete important parts of the operating system, bring poorly developed programs from home, or download conflicting or dangerous software packages from the Net.

"If your employees are currently downloading executable applications from the Internet and launching them on a computer on your network, your network is in danger. The firewall can be used to prevent the downloading of executable applications. When a software program is encountered on an FTP site, there is no way to verify that the program is what it claims to be. Recently, destructive programs have been found with the names of common shareware programs, such as PKZip 3.0, and Microsoft Word for Windows macros from reputable distributors have contained viruses. Netscape is an interesting example. It itself written in an unsafe language, and bastardized versions could make their way to FTP sites, yet it can handle Java applets within the safe Java subsystem, also known as a "sandbox."

Trusted Java

Act VII. In which the consultant explains how to play in the sandbox.

"How safe is this Java subsystem? While it is certainly safer to execute downloaded code produced and run within the Java Language Environment than binaries that were not designed from the ground up to be secure, both design and implementation flaws have led to attacks from the press and the creation of intentionally disruptive applets, as well as well-documented and well-reasoned questioning from the academic community. Netscape, a system written in an insecure language that runs Java applets, and HotJava, a system written from the ground up in Java, introduce different problems. The fact that Java will be embedded in the operating systems of most major vendors multiplies the concerns.

"The implementation of a corporate security policy requires the distinction between Java applets that are downloaded from trusted hosts, applets from untrusted hosts, unverifiable applets, and stand-alone, preloaded Java applications.

"At some point, certification authorities will issue keys to verify the source of an applet. That way, you will be able to set your browser configuration to accept only applets that have been tested and signed with an encrypted key. Before this happens, browser preferences can be set to allow applets to connect back only to the host from which they were downloaded, so that applets do not snoop for information within a network. With a digital signature, a user could guarantee that an applet is from a trusted source and has not been modified on its journey across the network. This would ultimately enable applets on the Internet to have the same functionality as stand-alone Java programs, unlimited by security restrictions.

"Securing an applet is similar to lobotomizing it. You limit its ability to function because you fear it will do damage. This fact makes Java a language much better suited for the corporate Intranet than for the Internet at large. Different browsers will implement security features in different ways. Some will make the defaults stringent; others will have a lax default restriction and count on the user to set an appropriate level of protection. There are plenty of reasons to want an applet to be able to write to a client computer's file system. At the end of a database query, the user might want to save the result on a local file. Or send it directly to a printer. There are also circumstances in which you would not want an applet to be able to read from or write to your local files, as the applet could do damage or gain restricted information for a third party.

"If you are developing applets or applications for a private or internal network, it makes sense to choose a browser with a less restrictive run-time environment. HotJava is being positioned as this type of application development and distribution environment. Netscape, by building in restrictive boundaries on applet behavior, will not be suitable for robust Intranet applications, but will be a good tool to use for surfing beyond the firewall. Fortunately, most implementations will be customized for your network and users. Let's take a look at the basic distinctions between what a downloaded applet is allowed to do, what a trusted applet can do, such as one that is read from the local file system, and what Java can do as a standalone application. This chart compares three scenarios: untrusted applet, trusted applet, and java application."

The consultant held up a chart:

TABLE 2.

Capabilities	Internet Applet	Intranet Applet	Java Application
Read local file	no	limited	yes
Write local file	no	limited	yes
Get file info	no	limited	yes
Delete file	no	no	yes
Read username or directory	no	limited	yes
Connect to port on client	no	limited	yes
Connect to port on originating host (server)	yes	yes	yes
Connect to port on third-party host	no	limited	yes
Load Java libraries	no	limited	yes
Quit interpreter	no	limited	yes
Create unannounced/unidentified pop-up window	no	yes	yes
Execute another program	no	limited	yes

"The rules guiding restrictions on applets will vary with implementation but generally follow common sense. You don't want an applet to pop up a window that looks like a word processor but secretly transmits your diary back over the Net. It must label itself as an "unsigned applet window." An applet cannot define its own SecurityManager object. It cannot define classes that are part of the packages of the local system or define system properties.

"Can these restrictions be circumvented? Under some circumstances, they can, but these will require elaborate spoofing mechanisms that undermine standard Internet protocols, such as the Domain Name Service. As a rule of thumb, if a network is connected, there is risk. Recovery procedures become more important than prevention, and you might decide that parts of your network should not be connected to parts that have Internet access. If the run-time system is fooled into believing that the applets came from a trusted host, such as the local-host, the run-time system will permit behaviors that should be restricted.

"Like a firewall that treats all networks outside the corporate confines as untrusted, the Java bytecode verifier that completes the loading process treats all Java code entering the system as untrusted and performs the equivalent of packet filtering, by challenging the code to prove that it was not constructed by a hostile compiler and that it will not try to perform illegal procedures. When bytecodes are accepted, they are still kept in a separate holding area, or "name space," where they are kept in a subsidiary position to built-in classes, unable to define or reference the system's packages. Just as firewalls and routers can theoretically be spoofed, or convinced that the attacker is sending packets from the inside, the Java security programs can only protect so much.

Automatic Garbage Collection

Act VI. In which the consultant talks trash.

"That fact that memory management is performed by the Java Virtual Machine rather than the programmer affects both speed of development and speed of execution. Besides making it difficult for a programmer to take advantage of memory allocation and referencing to disrupt a system, building memory management into the Java Virtual Machine specification makes the programmer's job much easier. In most languages, the programmer must explicitly request memory from the system and release memory segments when they are no longer needed. C programmers know what a pain in the rear malloc() is. For every object you create, you have to take steps to acquire memory space for it and explicitly release memory segments when you quit using them. With Java, the JVM handles all of that for you. It keeps track of which objects are no longer used and releases the memory automagically. Garbage collection runs in the background as a low-priority thread."

Threads

Act VII. In which the consultant spins a yarn.

"This boon to the programmer comes at some cost to the user. Because the applications are not hand-tooled to most efficiently use the specific system architecture, the programmer can compensate by managing how an application performs its various functions as separate, self-contained processes within the program. In many ways, threads are as difficult to manage as memory used to be.

"The fact that multithreading is built in at the language level in the run-time system and through thread objects makes the perceived performance of graphical applications that might need to stream in data, perform animations, respond to mouse events, and play audio much stronger without putting a lot more overhead on the local computer system. A thread runs as an efficient execution path while sharing the data area with other threads. Threads can have different priorities, be scheduled, perform maintenance roles in the background, and be suspended and resumed as needed.

Real-Time Java

Act VIII. In which the consultant gets real.

"With multithreading built into the language, interactive responsiveness is very good, about equivalent to what is perceived with applications that run directly on top of the operating system. There will be times, though, when high performance is required, and the sluggishness of an interpreted language will not be enough. Examples of applications that require high degrees of real-time performance:

- Applications that handle real-time input (stock market, radar, sonar, air traffic control)
- Videoconferencing and software decompression

- Multiplayer games
- Complex animations
- 3-D rendering
- Pen computing

"The main issue is that real-time garbage collection is significantly slower than hand-tooled memory management. The current, standard implementation from Sun is called mark-and-sweep, which performs at about half the efficiency of typical memory allocation systems. Many groups are working on improving the performance of Java, so that its benefits in development time and portability are matched by speed of execution.

"There are several options for improving performance:

1. Translate to native machine code at run-time (JIT compilers).
   Byte codes are translated on the fly to native machine code at runtime. Borland, Symantec and others have released JIT compilers that act as a drop-in replacement for Sun's run-time system. These are developed for a particular platform, but accept standard Java bytecode.

2. Have dedicated Java hardware (Java chips).
   Sun has announced three chips: PicoJava, MicroJAVA and UltraJAVA. PicoJAVA is a basic microcontroller, to be priced under $25. MicroJAVA is geared toward low-end games, telecom equipment and I/O controllers and will be priced at under $50. UltraJAVA will be targeted for NCs, game players, and 3D graphics, and priced at around $100. These can improve memory utilization efficiency and ease management.

3. Interface with other languages, such as C or C++, or hand-optimize memory management.
   Proprietary systems can be developed in languages other than Java that allow the programmer to allocate and schedule memory usage for particular tasks to enable real-time performance. An example would be a whiteboard with microphone that would use Java but

would also need to make system calls to use the microphone. The native method that would need to be called would require that the Java interface classes and dynamic-link library (DLL) be prein-stalled. Java can run an arbitrary executable written in any language, or call native C directly, to do something like read video off a local bus.

4. Create a lighter virtual machine
   Efforts such as NewMonics' PERC aim to achieve a real-time runtime system in part by relaxing the requirement that all class libraries be present in every Java Virtual Machine.

Business Logic

Act IX. In which the consultant spills the beans.

The consultant realized he had better get to the point, or risk losing his audience. The CEO said, "give us the bottom line. What's this gonna cost, and what are we going to get out of it?"

It seemed a bit backward to the consultant. He decided to ignore the question. Fortunately the COO intervened.

"You've heard our story. You've convinced us that Java is worth considering. Now how is this button of yours going to solve all our problems?" she said.

"What's the prognosis, doc?" said the CIO.

The consultant thought for a moment. "This is what I see," he said.

"There is a disjunction between the business logic of your organization, which runs on the central mission-critical systems, and the personal productivity software that runs on the desktop environment. You have expensive Pentium machines running word processing and spread-sheet software that loads off file servers. Some of these expensive desktop computers also have terminal emulators that provide a primitive window in which the user can manipulate data. Some of the more advanced, client-server solutions, help the user build database queries, but still require training, and if not properly implemented, can bring down the database. Word processors are becoming bloated with many functions, and features like "mail merging" require specialized expertise. In a fully object-oriented, distributed environment, pieces of software, such as a spell-checker, can be mixed and matched to provide functionality accross a wide variety of devices and applications. Word processors can have hooks into an inventory database, so that as your typing a letter, you can pull in product information. In Java, the database classes, text window classes, and networking classes are always available. Print catalog production can be customized down to a very closely targeted marked: each individual customer can receive a custom catalog. In each department and application there will be direct hooks into the business logic.

"So the main point is, start migrating to Java where you can now, and in the future, replace dumb terminals with Java terminals. In the short term, you can use a Java-based terminal emulation package, and slowly build in more functionality. Right now your corporation has embraced the Microsoft Windows API as a standard. If you begin to migrate toward Java, you can run applications on the Windows95 and NT platforms, and assure compatability with future devices and low-cost NCs, the new JavaOS and anything that supports the Java Virtual Machine. At some point, you will even be able to run legacy code, written in anything from C++ to ADA to COBOL on the JVM.

"Everyone is talking about open systems, Intranets and standards. Much of this is just public relations nonsense. But the concept of "write once, run anywhere" is important. Being able to mix and max blocks of object-oriented code will benefit your business, and make you less reliant on monolithic "office" or "groupware" packages. Any of the applications we reviewed can benefit from these features of Java.

"When will Java applications be available? When will NCs be ready for prime time? Will competing network operating systems and programming languages, such as Lucent's Inferno platform, eclipse Java? These are difficult questions to answer. It will be hard to imagine a successful system being launched that cannot support the JVM. Java applets and applications will most likely be able to run on systems that are perceived to compete with Java. Today, the JVM provides a platform that we can begin using to move away from two types of systems that we know will not succeed for the agile, responsive business in the long run: centrally-administered mainframe and client/server."

## CHAPTER 21

Data Mining on the Intranet, Electronic Commerce on the Internet

"The idea of Java chips, or dedicated Java gear, brings up the issue of performance verses openness. It seems to contradict the idea of a Virtual Machine if it's cast in silicon. The success of the Internet is based on the fact that all pieces can interoperate, as it is based on standards produced by discussions of the Internet Engineering Task Force (IETF).

"The success of the Internet has led companies to rethink their corporate networks, moving from proprietary protocols like Apple's Appletalk, Novell's IPX/SPX, Digital's DECNET and Microsoft's NetBeui, to pure TCP/IP. By separating the protocol layer from the operating system, and leaping right up to the application level, users are finding interoperability across platforms and between corporations. Anyone can FTP a file to a commonly reachable host and use FTP to retrieve a file. Anyone can use a browser to locate information or Telnet to login to a common host and have a talk session. The useful applications become rooted in the network, rather than the operating system.

"Companies are taking advantage of the explosion of software developed for TCP/IP by creating Intranets, or private TCP/IP networks, that give users the ability to connect to systems located at other institutions by routing over the Internet or through private or "virtual private" networks. The fact that Novell, Microsoft, IBM, Tandem, and others have licensed Java to embed in their operating systems and network operating systems (NOS), makes the Intranet a powerful tool for sharing applications as well as information and communications. Eventually, applications themselves will be fragmented and modular, and flow through the network as easily as protocols.

"While closed systems may perform better, as all the physical network, protocol, operating systems, hardware and applications are optimized for one-another, an open system allows greater flexibility and the ability to take advantage of innovations. A single vendor cannot develop or maintain a proprietary suite as easily as a universe of scientists, students, administrators and programmers working on developing based on public specifications. It is expected that the earnings of the sum of the small software houses that are just now starting up will, within 10 years, eclipse the earnings Microsoft and other software giants.

"How does a corporation take advantage of this? For one, hollow out the PC . Network managers are looking to return to the day of the mainframe and dumb terminals for the ease of network and systems management. Users love their PCs and want to control the interface and applications. Network Computer (NCs) give the best of both worlds: a centrally managed system with central software distribution, as well as state-of-the-art GUI and client-server applications.

"The NC loads the HotJava browser as its default environment, primarily as a way for the user to quickly locate applets and other applications from around the network. Calendar programs, for example, can be stored on a central server and loaded as needed. The difference between a calendar program written in Java and traditional time management applications that communicate or load over a network is that it is modular. It can be readily incorporated into any document or other application. It can be attached to a task-flow or project-management designer, an employee history database, or an accounting package. It can share classes and form a suite of applications on the spot. Most important, the data is not locked into the application, or on the desktop, so can be shared with other users and be utilized by other applications.

"Another important feature is remote access. When a user goes home to a PC running Java, applets can be loaded over the Internet or through dial-up PPP or ISDN connections to the corporate network. The user does not need to duplicate an application suite when on the road with a laptop or at a remote office. All the pieces are small, but the total capability is large.

"Data Mining and Data Warehousing enable the end user to formulate their database queries. Data Warehouses are Decision Support Systems (DSS) and consist of information information extracted from Online Transaction Processing systems (OLTP). Java database front ends are a perfect utility for putting data manipulation capabilities into the hands of the end user, highly customizing the end user's environment so that searches are fruitful, and tying data-mining operations into other desktop applications."

The Java Database Connectivity Specification

The consultant paused. The executives were silent. "Right," he said. "The button. I was explaining the concept of just one button.

"We want to design a system that is centrally managed, but all capabilities and information are available at the periphery. Access control is crucial. Vendors, customers, tech support, sales reps, management, and partners all need different things from the same system. So the first thing the system needs to determine is: who the user is, and what do they want.

"We are already starting to think about databases. Relating information to a particular key individual. The button is pressed. A dialog box appears. The user enters a name and password. Through a socket connection, this information is transferred to a database and more Java classes are loaded: e-mail client, bulletin boards, word processing, database entry forms or query forms, depending on the role and needs of the user. If it's a third party, such as the retailer we discussed above, the user could get new messages with new product layout rendering that would automatically display, since they were sent with a small binary applet.

"The database, or Data Warehouse, as the central repository of the enterprise has come to be called, is the focal point of the network. Users are demanding more and more data be available at their fingertips at any time for decision support. Java has a clear advantage as a database front-end development tool, as it is modular and easily customized for a particular purpose. Interfaces targeted at a particular user can be distributed to the user from the actual database.

"The Java Database Connectivity (JDBC) specification is leading a standardization and interoperability process that promises to create a vendor-independent means of achieving access to relational databases. The JDBC provides a basic, low-level API for SQL (Structured Query Language) functions, so that higher level database access tools can be built. The JDBC is similar to the ODBC (Microsoft's Open Database Connectivity), in that both were based on the X/Open's SQL CLI (Call Level Interface). The similarity to ODBC will aid in the adoption of JDBC, yet it does not rely on calling the ODBC directly to function.

"The JDBC will allow for the development of easy-to-use interfaces over the Internet and Intranets that are platform independent and maintain socket connections to the database server as information is being passed and processed. This is an extension of and expansion on Web-based database query tools that use PERL CGI gateways, pro*c or PL/SQL in stored procedures to generate HTML on the fly for display in the Web browser.

"By building the front end in Java, rather than HTML, the communication with the database server can be bidirectional. HTTP does not support sessions, it simply gets a query and posts data. Interactivity should not require a constant rebuilding of web pages and reestablishing connections. For example, in watching weather maps, sports, or stock information, the database should not have to be requeried and rebuilt to see each data point or any other changes.

"The JDBC API is a series of Java interfaces that allow a programmer to implement Java applications and applets that:

1. open database connections
2. execute statements
3. process the results

"The abstract interfaces that are used to achieve this include:

- java.sql.DriverManager to support the creation of new connections
- java.sql.Connection to represent a connection to a particular database
- java.sql.Statement which acts as a container for executing a particular SQL statement on a connection
- java.sql.ResultSet to control access to the row results of a given SQL statement

"While Java and JDBC opens up a world of new possibilities for distributing and receiving data through the Internet and over the Enterprise, the heterogeneous and distributed terrain requires security measures and naming conventions to assure that the user will locate the correct data and database and that integrity is maintained.

"On private LANs, databases can be specified by PERSONNEL or RECORDS, with the full path to the service preloaded in an INI file or in the application that uses ODBC. On the Internet, fully qualified

URLs are used to locate resources. JDBC can be used in several scenarios:

1. Applets, which will need the fully qualified URL to connect back to the host machine from which it was distributed. Untrusted applets will not be allowed to write to the local file system, so data cannot be saved and stored locally. Performance will differ depending on Internet congestion and latency. The SecurityManager in the java.lang package can monitor connections and throw exceptions if illegal connections are attempted.

2. Applications, which can function exactly like platform-specific applications that use other SQL drivers. They resolve abbreviated identifiers, such as CUSTOMERS or STOCK, by storing the fully qualified database location locally.

3. Middleware, such as SunSoft's *Joe*, can be called, rather than connecting directly between the Java front end and the database. With Joe, a few lines can be added to the Java code to call an Object Request Broker (ORB) through a Remote Procedure Call (RPC) or socket. The ORB's Interface Definition Language (IDL) handles the communication with the database and the communication with the Java applet or application. Precompiled C++ objects live on object servers around the network with built-in operations that can be easily called with Java stubs. This might be a more industrial grade solution for the Intranet.

"JDBC uses the Web's URL syntax of:

protocol://host.domain.service:port/directory/subdirectory/name

For example:

jdbc://www.pentagon.net:1542/cds/classical

would connect to the classical music database at Pentagon CDs and Tapes. If a subprotocol is used, such as ODBC, or if a new protocol, such as MoonBean (mb), is used to make the final database connection to the database, in this case named Spot, the URL would be:

jdbc:mb://iron.butterfly.net:8888/community

"This type of request can be embedded in a Java button, much as a URL appears as a hypertext link so that the user does not need to enter it in the browser window.

URLs to URIs and URNs

"Increased database use on the Internet will make the location of discrete "pages" less clear-cut. Content is generated dynamically, rather than stored as a concrete file at a specific location. Allowing an Internet user to indicate a particular resource, rather than specifying its location, has been under development and discussion by the IETF and the World Wide Web Consortium. Uniform Resource Names (URNs) would be a short string that would refer to an object on the Web, such as Joe's Winter Poem, rather than http://www.clark.net/~joe/poems/earlywork/winter.html. URNs would be resolved by a new type of name service, so that an object could that persist beyond the fluctuations of domain names and hosts could still be found. Universal Resource Identifiers (URIs) are the set of all URLs and URNs.

"By identifying a naming service on a network, the JDBC can move the Internet closer to a URN system. Here, the protocol, naming service, and database are identified:

```
jdbc:mbnaming:SpotsBar
```

"The MoonBean naming server on the local network would direct the query that could have come in from anywhere to the host where the SpotsBar database resides. New subprotocols, such as MoonBean, can be registered and reserved by JavaSoft.

The currently defined JDBC core Java interfaces and classes are:

- java.sql.CallableStatement
- java.sql.Connection
- java.sql.DataTruncation
- java.sql.Date
- java.sql.driver
- java.sql.Drivermanager
- Java.sql.NullData
- java.sql.Numericjava.sql.PreparedStatement
- java.sql.ResultSet
- java.sql.SQLException
- java.sql.SQLWarning
- java.sql.Statement
- java.sql.Time
- java.sql.Timestamp
- java.sql.Types

Data types supported in JDBC:

SQL	Java
CHAR	String
VARCHAR	String
LONGVARCHAR	java.io.InputStream
NUMERIC	java.sql.Numeric
DECIMAL	java.sql.Numeric
BIT	boolean
TINYINT	byte
SMALLINT	short
INTEGER	int
BIGINT	long
REAL	float
FLOAT	float

```
DOUBLE           double
BINARY           byte[]
VARBINARY        byte[]
LONGVARBINARY    java.io.InputStream
DATE             java.sql.Date
TIME             java.sql.Time
TIMESTAMP        java.sql.Timestamp
```

"When a connection is opened, a java.util.Properties object can be passed to map between tag and value strings. Username and Password can be passed this way. Because Java is inherently multi-threaded, it can begin building the user interface, start up database operations and handle other work simultaneously. Multithreading also allow multiple Statements on the same Connection to be processed simultaneously and ResultSets retrieved.

"Just as segments of C code can be stored in a database for execution within the database environment, to be processed like any other SQL statement, Java code for use by the end user can now be stored. Database applications are now designed to take advantage of stored procedures, and they will soon be designed to take advantage of stored Java code, which is significantly different from text or media binary files.

Strategic Java Deployment

"Data warehousing is saving businesses billions of dollars a year, as centrally managed stores of information are more easily maintained than databases distributed over multiple systems and platforms. When different types of information, for example, customer demographics, employee records, and sales data, are stored in one database, the information can also be related in new ways to produce unique perspectives on the performance of individuals, teams, and the organization as a whole.

"By storing applications (or applets) in the database along with media files, records, and procedures, a company can cut down on the cost of client computers, that are requiring ever faster processors and more RAM to run software for an increasing number of features. An application with more features than are required by an average user is called "bloatware." Microsoft Word 6.0, for example, took several minutes to load on a Macintosh, requiring that users leave it running on the desktop, which stole RAM from other applications. The advanced features of Word were rarely used and did not need to be taking up system resources.

A word processing program written in Java could be stored in the database as modular text fields, drawing programs, search and replace, templates, and spell checkers. Each of these components, being very small, can load over the network in the background when an applet is launched, or can be pulled on request. The components can be mixed and matched for other applications, such as the preparation of custom mailings and catalogs. The fact that the customer data and technical specifications are stored in the same data warehouse will make word processing and mail-merge applications available with preloaded documents, addresses and graphics.

"Many companies are beginning to use SGML to produce catalogs and manuals from relational databases. A catalog publishing system could work like this:

- An SGML DTD is defined to describe the elements of the database (such as <ILLUS>, <SUBHEAD>, <BRAND>, <COLOR>, <MODEL>, <DESCRIPTION>, <PRICE>).
- Procedural code is stored in the database to insert a particular price depending on a primary key, such as a customer code. Certain customers would get "LIST" or "SCHEDA" or "SCHEDB" prices, but the layout of the catalog, the columns, type, etc. would remain consistent. An exchange rate could be factored in. A custom catalog could be produced with all red products or all products under

$2,000. When a report is produced from a query, the formatted text is produced on the fly.

- An interface with a publishing package such as FrameMaker or InterLeaf generates output formatted in postscript, with graphics, columns, tables,and other presentation elements. This is sent to a printer over the network. Adobe's portable 2-D imaging model, currently named Bravo, has been licensed by JavaSoft to provide advanced layout capabilities for Java applets and applications.

"If you use HTML as the SGML DTD and send the report over the Internet or Intranet to a browser, you have a solid base for an enterprise information and electronic commerce service. Already, a large portion of the professional content on the Web is HTML that has been generated on the fly from databases, rather than stored as flat files. Oracle, Netscape, Microsoft and many others have productized database/Webserver bundles. As explained, current Web applications consist of an HTML forms-based interface and a CGI script of program. The growth of Web-based database interfaces suggests that this is a useful approach. The downsides have already been addressed:

- A limited user interface: static, without drag-and-drop capabilities and other familiar controls.
- Contact with the database is through HTTP commands "GET" and "PUT," which does not support real-time data streams, so screen updates are wholesale page replacements that displace the data from the context.
- User input through CGI scripts is reduced to strings that have to be parsed and processed back into primitive data types, either in the script or with additional database procedures.

"HTML is essentially a legacy solution. It is a particular SGML DTD that is useful in conjunction with HTTP for navigating through archives of documents and presenting static content. Attempts to make it "engaging" generally result in cute gimcrackery or sites that become dysfunctional under the weight of icons, frames and background colors. Embedding PDF (Adobe's Printer Description Format) documents, improving font and other presentation capabilities, extending HTML is a limited and short-sighted attempt to give Web content the sign of professionalism and permanence, by adopting the trappings of print layout. Institutions want their corporate presentation to appear set in stone, solid, and lasting. Media companies want their Web presence to reflect a big budget.

"The problem is that it is not expensive to produce or distribute content on the Internet, and the more the content presentation is predefined, the less flexible it is, or useful over time. The form should, and ultimately must, follow the function. Just as typefaces and other print layout conventions arose to communicate a context to accompany the content, new electronic presentation formats will be geared to aid interaction and change over time. The GET/PUT/REPLACE of HTTP, with successive screens and links, is being replaced with a more seamless, dynamic shifting of content and context. The flat computer screen is becoming populated with active voices in often slapstick interactivity. The idea of presenting content on the computer screen, the digital archive or electronic library, is becoming as anachronistic as the horseless carriage. The car is a new animal, as is the networked computer.

Java can be used to build flexible front ends, such as SGML browsers that load a DTD along with the data, or presentation classes specific to a document, or stored with the data in the database. The return set can be sent to a printer, stored in a file on the client computer, stored on the server in a reserved directory, used for further analysis. The nature of data, though, is that it is dynamic. The procedures, activities, relationships, objects and tools are over the long term more important than any particular document. At some point, the link between printed reports and networked information systems will be severed, and they will become two completely separate media. Already Motorola and other technology companies are putting annual reports on the Web and not publishing printed versions. If the data is available, and the presentation language and network is in place to have that annual report updated to the minute, time becomes very important part of the data structure. The Bloomberg is becoming ubiquitous.

The Java Electronic Commerce Framework

"The Java Electronic Commerce Framework (JECF) was devised to address basic issues of a distributed transaction environment. While its central mission is to standardize Internet shopping, the JECF also offers solutions to problems of interoperability over any heterogenous network such as the corporate Intranet.

"Where the systems industry is at odds on issues such as directory services and access-control standards, the JECF can function as a unifying force. Many Internet and Intranet vendors, such as Netscape and Novell, are supporting the Lightweight Directorty Access Protocol (LDAP) over the older X.500 standard. As vendors add support for LDAP, users will able to maintain a single username and password across databases, applications and networks. In encryption and user authentication, the JECF currently supports the Secure Electronic Transactions (SET) protocol and will most likely support the X.509 digital encryption standard, as well as SSL and S-HTTP as extensions to the basic security features of the Java kernel.

"The following security features of Java 1.0 and Java 1.1 are utilized by the JECF:

- Signed applets

  Applets can be digitally signed so that they can perform operations that would not be allowed of untrusted applets.
- Code verification

  The Java compiled bytecode is inspected to ensure that it conforms to the runtime rules of the Java Language Specification.

The JECF extends the basic security features to provide many other components, including the following:

- User identification

  A unique user name in the JECF environment with separate databases for multiple users sharing a single computer, with the option for a more global registry.

- User authentication

  Password validation is performed locally so that passwords are never sent over the network where they can be intercepted.

- User authorization and access control

  Certain applications will be visible and available only to specified users once they are validated. Access control lists specify which database objects are available to an authenticated user.

- Version control

  Version numbers are included in classes that are loaded over the network to ensure that the correct version is used.

"The applications of the Java Electronic Commerce Framework are evident. Java can be used in:

- Smart cards
- Credit and debit cards
- Micropayments for information or multiplayer games
- Banking
- Brokerage
- Tax reporting
- Coupons
- Internet retailing
- Point of sale
- Intranet applications

"Remote-access and third-party connectivity will be greatly enhanced by JECF mechanisms. For example, advertising agencies can access portions of a corporate database to check sales against advertisement dollars spent in a region. Retailers and distributors can gain limited access to a manufactureres product database. Customers can gain access to their account information and track the order-fulfillment process."

GroupWhere

"A very important element of the business information systems that has not been adequately supported by Internet and Intranet technologies is truly dynamic, or even real-time, collaborative environments. The Web can provide an interface to an archive of asynchronous, multiuser communications systems, such as HyperMail for mailing lists or Netscape's News Server for usenet-style discussion groups. It can act as a bulletin board system (BBS) for posting and threading conversations. It can include hypertext references for other documents on the Net to serve as annotations to a thread, but the Web has not been able to join these services to real-time communal conferencing environments.

"Business is not always asynchronous. There are many times when conversations need to take place, and phone conversations are not always the most efficient means of communicating, particularly with multiple parties. Since its founding, HuskyLabs' MOO has been the true office environment where programmers, designers and even customers meet, socialize, collaborate and interact. By building in shared whiteboard spaces, word processors, presentation layers and audiovisual support, dynamic documents are created based on the state of the objects within the system.

"With Internet telephony and other accoutrements, a live object database will be an essential business tool. Already, the interaction with the computer is becoming as central to the business day as the interaction with the phone. The gesture of pushing notions into cyberspace through the keyboard and mouse, reacting to messages from other persons on the network, funneling information where it should go, requesting information from live librarians and associates will ultimately be more a part of the business day than searching through databases, text-retrieval engines and archives. It is important to remember that the mouth and throat used for guttural pronoucements are a repurposing of organs for chewing and swallowing. Typing is no less natural than speech, and the act of taking notes is built right into the conversation. As MOOs grow up and get real, we also find that databases aren't just for storage and retrieval of business information, but can also be used for real-time collaboration and communication between the database objects."

The consultant turns on a projector connected to his laptop which is jacked into the Net and demonstrates the advanced applications covered in the next section.

IV. Immersive Java

"The computer can't tell you the emotional story.
It can give you the exact mathematical design,
but what's missing is the eyebrows."
—Frank Zappa

## CHAPTER 22

Server-side Java

While the benefits of Java and the Java Virtual Machine are most evident on the desktop, interesting things can be done with Java in the Web or database server. HTTP servers are available written in Java with objects that function as extensible modules to perform functions traditionally relegated to CGI. Most high-performance server-side systems will be developed using CORBA-compliant C++ code and other platform-dependent languages, Java's multithreaded nature and built-in memory management make it a nice language for prototyping and rapidly deploying server-based software.

The HistoryServer and HistoryApplet

This example includes "history server" software that records impressions created by an applet distributed from the Web server running on history server host. Every time a page with the applet is loaded or reloaded, the date, time and hostname of the the access is recorded by the history server and displayed remotely in the applet window.

```
http://www.lab.com/LiveJava/developers/HistorySer-
ver.html
```

The history server is an application, and the history client is an applet. The source code is comprised of the following two files:

- **HistoryServer.java** which contains the server application.
- **HistoryApplet.java** that contains the client applet.

The applet is, by definition, distributed with a Web page embedded in HTML with an <applet> tag. Example usage is given at the top of the HTML source file.

The application is started with

```
java HistoryServer [port]
```

at the command line of the server. This can be accomplished automatically at regular intervals through a "cron job" or by the Web server through a prespecified stimulus. The default port to which the history server listens is 7425 if no port is specified on the command line. Java applications are always started by invoking the Java run-time system by name.

The HistoryServer is a basic example in implementing ServerSockets in Java. It demonstates the use of ServerSocket.accept() to accept an incoming socket and perform IO on the established connection.

The Server

The HistoryServer contains an instance of the java.net.ServerSocket class. The most important feature of the ServerSocket class is the accept() method, which accepts an incoming connection. The History-Server waits for a connection (by calling accept()) and then, depending on the information read from the socket, either records a new hit (to the file .hithistory on the server) or prints out the existing history information. After its simple task, the socket is closed and the server waits for a new connection.

The same HistoryServer and .hithistory file can be used for any number of web pages. The HistoryApplet and HistoryServer are smart enough to know what URL is logging or requesting history info.

```
/*
 * @(#)HistoryServer.java1.0b1 04/07/96 sick@butterfly.net
 * written by Michael Reece
 * contains the HistoryServer application
 *
 */
```

```
/*
```

This is an application, not an applet. Run the compiled class with:

java HistoryServer.

An optional argument defines the port to listen to. The default is 7425. The HistoryServer will listen to the port and wait for connections from a History Applet. When a connection is made, it can request to LOG a new entry, or LIST the existing history.

```
*/
```

```
import java.net.*;
import java.io.*;
import java.util.*;
```

```
/**
 * the HistoryServer application
 */
public class HistoryServer {
```

```java
static String HELLO = "Hello?";   // HistoryApplet will send
// this
static String REPLY = "Hello!";   // and HistoryServer will
// respond with this

static String LOGNAME = ".hithistory";  // local file where
// data is stored

static ServerSocket server = null;  // the server socket
static int port = 7425;             // port to listen to


/**
 * main application code. sets up the server and listens for
 *    connections
 * forever
 */
public static void main(String args[]) {

  Socket socket;  // an incoming socket

  // check for command line argument
  if (args.length > 0) port = Integer.parseInt(args[0]);

  System.out.println("Opening ServerSocket on port " + port
    + " ...");
  try {
    server = new ServerSocket(port);
  } catch (Exception e) {
    System.out.println("Exception: " + e);
    System.exit(1);
  }

  while (true) {
    System.out.println("Waiting for connection ...");
    try {
      socket = server.accept();
      System.out.println("Connection accepted!");
      handleSocket(socket);
    } catch (Exception e) {
      System.out.println("Exception: " + e);
      System.exit(1);
    }
```

```
    }

  }


  /**
   * here's where the meaty stuff is
   */
  public static void handleSocket(Socket socket) {
    DataInputStream istream = null;   // socket's input stream
    PrintStream ostream = null;       // socket's output stream
    String who;                       // who is connecting

    String line;
    boolean valid = false;
    int i;

    try {
      istream = new DataInputStream(
        new BufferedInputStream(socket.getInputStream()));
      ostream = new PrintStream(
        new BufferedOutputStream(socket.getOutputStream()),
                  true);
    } catch (Exception e) {
      System.out.println("Exception: " + e);
    }

    // see who this is
    who = socket.getInetAddress().getHostName();
    i = who.indexOf("/");
    if (i  > 0) who = who.substring(0, i);
    System.out.println("  Who: " + who);

    // establish handshaking
    try {
      String hello = istream.readLine();
      System.out.println("  Received: " + hello);
      if (hello.equals(HELLO)) {
        System.out.println("  Sending: " + REPLY);
        ostream.println(REPLY);
        valid = true;
      } else {
        System.out.println("  Bogus handshake.");
```

```
    }
  } catch (Exception e) {
    System.out.println("Exception: " + e);
  }

  // listen for a command from the socket
  if (valid) {
    try {
      line = istream.readLine();
      System.out.println("  Received: " + line);
      if (line.startsWith("LOG ")) {  // log this hit
        String url = line.substring(4);
        System.out.println("    url: <" + url + ">");
        addHistory(url, who);
      } else if (line.startsWith("LIST ")) {  // find the
        // hits
        i = line.indexOf(",", 5);
        String url = line.substring(5, i);
        int len = Integer.parseInt(line.substring(i+1));
        System.out.println("    url: <" + url + ">");
        System.out.println("    len: <" + len + ">");
        String hist[] = getHistory(url, len);
        for (i = 0; i < hist.length; i++) {
          System.out.println("  Sending: " + hist[i]);
          ostream.println(hist[i]);
        }

      } else {
        System.out.println("  Bogus command.");
      }
    } catch (Exception e) {
      System.out.println("Exception: " + e);
    }
  }

  System.out.println("Closing connection.");
  try {
    socket.close();
  } catch (Exception e) {
    System.out.println("Exception: " + e);
  }

}
```

```
/**
 * add a history entry for this hit, writing the log
 *  'backwards' by first
 * reading in the existing text and appending it to the end
 *   of the current
 * entry, then put it all back in the file
 * @param url the url being hit
 * @param who the host hitting the url
 */
public static void addHistory(String url, String who) {
  String date = getDate();
  String line;

  // this will be the finished result, start with current hit
  // at front
  String newtext = (url + "," + date + "," + who + "\n");

  // read existing text and append it to the new text
  try {
    DataInputStream ifile = new DataInputStream(
      new FileInputStream(LOGNAME));
    while ((line = ifile.readLine()) != null) newtext +=
      (line + "\n");
    ifile.close();
  } catch (FileNotFoundException e) {
    System.out.println(LOGNAME + " does not exist.");
  } catch (Exception e) {
    System.out.println("Reading " + LOGNAME + ": " + e);
    return;
  }

  // now open the file for writing, and put the new text back
  // in
  try {
    PrintStream ofile = new PrintStream(
        new FileOutputStream(LOGNAME));
    ofile.print(newtext);
    ofile.close();
  } catch (Exception e) {
    System.out.println("Writing " + LOGNAME + ": " + e);
  }
}
```

```java
/**
 * open the log and pull out the most recent hits for the url
 * @param url the url to find hits on
 * @param len the number of hits to return
 */
public static String[] getHistory(String url, int len) {
    String hist[] = new String[len];
    int num = 0;
    String line;

    // open the file
    try {
        DataInputStream ifile = new DataInputStream(
            new FileInputStream(LOGNAME));
        // keep reading until we have enough or reach the end
        while ((num < len) && ((line = ifile.readLine()) !=
            null)) {
            int i = line.indexOf(",");
            // see if this is the right url
            if (line.substring(0, i).equals(url)) {
                // yep! add it to the list
                hist[num] = line.substring(i+1);
                num++;
            }
        }
        ifile.close();
    } catch (Exception e) {
        System.out.println("Reading " + LOGNAME + ": " + e);
    }

    // filler for urls with few hits
    for ( ; num < len; num++) hist[num] = "    (none)   ,
        (pre-history)";

    return hist;
}


/**
 * get the current data and time in the form "hh:mm MM/DD"
 */
```

```
public static String getDate() {
  Date d = new Date();

  return padInt(d.getHours()) + ":" + padInt(d.getMinutes())
  + " " + padInt(d.getMonth()+1) + "/" + padInt(d.getDate());
}


/**
  * convert the int to a String, and stick a '0' in front if
  *    it's <10
  */
public static String padInt(int i) {
  return ((i < 10) ? "0" : "") + String.valueOf(i);
}
```

The History Client

The HistoryApplet is the client that communicates with the server. When started, it initiates a connection to the history server and logs the new hit. Once that connection is closed, a new connection is opened to read history info from the server. The history information is displayed in a HistoryList object, which is an enhanced java.awt.List class.

A sample Web page for distribution of the applet follows:

```
<html>
<head>
<title>HistoryApplet test page</title>
</head>

<body>

<center>
<h2> History </h2>
<hr>
<applet code="HistoryApplet.class" width=500 height=180>
<param name="histlen" value="10">
```

```
</applet>
</center>

<hr>
<address>
<a href="mailto:sick@butterfly.net">sick@butterfly.net</a>
</address>
</body>
</html>
```

The applet source code follows:

```
/*
 * @(#)HistoryApplet.java1.0b1 04/07/96 sick@butterfly.net
 *
 * contains the HistoryApplet and HistoryList classes
 *
 */

/*
Optional <params> for the <applet> tag:

  thisurl—the url for the .html file. If not provided, get
  DocumentBase() is used.

  histserver—the the host where the HistoryServer is
  located.If not provided, getDocumentBase().getHost() is
  used.

  histport—the port the HistoryServer is listening to.
  Default is 7425.

  histlen—the number of history entries to be displayed.
  Default is 10.

Example <applet> tag:

  <applet code="HistoryApplet.class" width=410 height=160>

  <param name="histlen" value="20">

  </applet>
```

```
*/

import java.applet.*;
import java.net.*;
import java.io.*;
import java.awt.*;

/**
 * the HistoryApplet connects to the HistoryServer to update
 *   and read history
 * log info.
 */
public class HistoryApplet extends Applet {

  String HELLO = "Hello?";  // sent to the HistoryServer for
  // handshaking
  String REPLY = "Hello!";  // expected reply from the
  // HistoryServer

  String thisurl = "";      // the url for the page containing
  // this applet
  String histserver = "";    // the host where the HistoryServer
  // is found
  int histport = 7425;       // the port the HistoryServer is
  // listening to
  int histlen = 10;          // number of history items to
  // display

  HistoryList history = null;  // the list history items, see
  // HistoryList class

  Socket socket = null;              // the socket used to connect
  // to the server
  DataInputStream istream = null;  // the socket's input stream
  PrintStream ostream = null;      // the socket's output
  // stream


  /**
   * initialize the applet, reading in any <param> values and
   *   setting up the
   * history list
   */
  public void init() {
```

```
    String p;

    if ((p = getParameter("thisurl")) != null) thisurl = p;
    else thisurl = getDocumentBase().toString();

    // if the url ends with a slash, append 'index.html' to the
    //   end so "/path/"
    // and "/path/index.html" are synonymous
    if (thisurl.endsWith("/")) thisurl += "index.html";

    if ((p = getParameter("histserver")) != null)  histserver
      = p;
    else histserver = getDocumentBase().getHost();

    if ((p = getParameter("histport")) != null)  histport =
      Integer.parseInt(p);

    if ((p = getParameter("histlen")) != null)
    histlen = Inte ger.parseInt(p);

    // set up a fixed-space font so the history list lines up
    // nicely
    Font f = new Font("Courier", Font.PLAIN, 10);
    if (f != null) setFont(f);

    history = new HistoryList(histlen);
    this.add(history);
  }


/**
 * start the applet. this logs the current 'hit' and reads in
 *    the history
 */
public void start() {
  logHistory();
  getHistory();
}


/**
 * connect to the HistoryServer and log this hit
```

```
 */
public void logHistory() {
  if (connect()) {
    ostream.println("LOG " + thisurl);
    disconnect();
  } else {
    history.addItem("Error:", "Unable to log history.");
  }
}


/**
 * connect to the HistoryServer and read in the history list
 */
public void getHistory() {
  if (connect()) {
    history.resetList();
    ostream.println("LIST " + thisurl + "," + histlen);

    try {
      int num = 0, i;
      String line;
      while ((num < histlen) && ((line = istream.readLine())
        != null)) {
        // line should be "date,who" -- but just in case...
        if ((i = line.indexOf(",")) > 0)
          history.addItem(line.substring(0,i),
          line.substring(i+1));
        else
          history.addItem("Bad line:", line);

        num++;
      }
    } catch (Exception e) {
      history.addItem("Error:", "Exception reading
        history.");
    }

    disconnect();
  } else {
    history.addItem("Error:", "Unable to read history.");
  }
```

```
        }


        /**
         * connect to the HistoryServer and establish handshaking.
         * @returns true on success
         */
        public boolean connect() {
          try {
            socket = new Socket(histserver, histport);
            istream = new DataInputStream(
              new BufferedInputStream(socket.getInputStream()));
            ostream = new PrintStream(
              new BufferedOutputStream(socket.getOutput  Stream()),true);

            System.out.println("HistoryApplet.connect: sending \"" +
              HELLO + "\"");
            ostream.println(HELLO);

            String line = istream.readLine();
            System.out.println("HistoryApplet.connect: received \""
              + line + "\"");
            if (line.equals(REPLY)) return true;   // success!

          } catch (Exception e) {
            System.out.println("HistoryApplet.connect: " + e);
          }
          return false;
        }


        /**
         * disconect the socket to the HistoryServer
         */
        public void disconnect() {
          if (socket != null) {
            try {
              socket.close();
            } catch (Exception ignored) {
            }
            socket = null;
          }
```

```
    }

}



/**
 * a subclass of java.awt.List to make my life simpler.
 */
class HistoryList extends List {

  /**
   * the width of the list box.  after trying unsuccessfully to
   *   get a standard
   * List object to change its size, i decided i'd just over
   *   ride the size.
   */
  public int listWidth = 400;

  /**
   * constructs a new HistoryList with the specified rows, plus
   *   one for the
   * header
   * @param rows the number of items you wish to display
   *   beneath the header
   */
  public HistoryList(int rows) {
    super(rows + 2, false);
    this.resetList();
  }


  /**
   * return the preferred size for the history list, making use
   *   of the listWidth
   * defined above
   */
  public Dimension preferredSize() {
    Dimension d = super.preferredSize();
    d.width = this.listWidth;
    return d;
  }
```

```
/**
 * returns preferredSize(), since that's is what i consider
 *    the minimum
 */
public Dimension minimumSize() {
  return preferredSize();
}



/**
 * this is a matter of convenience. the date and host are
 *    concatenated and
 * passed to the inherited addItem as a single string
 */
public void addItem(String date, String host) {
  while (date.length() < 11) date += " ";
  super.addItem(date + "   " + host);
}



/**
 * reset the list by clearing out the existing items and
 * starting over with
 * the header in place
 */
public void resetList() {
  this.delItems(0, this.countItems()-1);
  this.addItem("time   date",   "hostname");
  this.addItem("-----------", "-----------------------------
  --------");
}

}
```

## CHAPTER 23

Database to Interface: The Front End

VRML: Cyberspace as a MIME-type

Virtual Reality Modeling Language (VRML) was designed to create a spatial arrangement for the media and text objects located on a system or network. The thinking was that URLs are difficult to remember. Try telling your grandmother to look at the new baby pictures on http://www.kansasnet.com:8080/pub/users/joseph/baby/marsha16mo.html. It would be much easier to tell her that the baby pictures are located on the refrigerator door, in the kitchen of our new home page in Virtual Kansas. She could cruise over to virtual Kansas with the mouse, sweep straight into the house, and click the photos right off the 'fridge.

In practice, though, navigating spacially is no easier than clicking through hierarchies of text links. VRML has imported all the problems of the real world into cyberspace. How do we get from here to there? When I get to Kansas, how do I know which housing development to approach? What's grandma's street address? The houses all look the same! Getting around a virtual New York, with all the shops, goods, agencies, signs, documents and people, would be more difficult than navigating the real thing. One quickly realizes that people already have a profound ability for abstraction. Rendered objects, texture maps, shadows and light sources provide a false sense of familiarity by playing on the human capacity for visualization but do not help someone remember where a media or text object is located or help them to retrieve it. It also does not aid significantly in the understanding or appreciation of the message or concept.

This literalization of cyberspace runs counter to the human tendency toward abstraction, which enables humans to encode and encapsulate ideas in ever briefer significations so as to build ever more elaborate complexes of meaning. Take the sign on the women's room as an example. It is a circle, a triangle, and a square, put together to represent a woman in a dress. You know it means that this is a place for a woman to go to relieve herself. The sign does not have to show the woman peeing. It certainly doesn't have to show a well-rendered woman with a flowing, calico dress, drop shadows and animations. The sign could just as easily have said "Women."

With VRML worlds, there is a blurred distinction between a signifier and a sign. Is the helicopter with the whirring blades a link to an archive of helicopter photos? Is the helicopter the thing in itself, to be manipulated with the mouse or enlarged to provide details of the cockpit? Could the information have been conveyed as easily with a button labeled "helicopter."

On VRML discussion groups, there is generally a great deal of arguing about the best way to represent a chair, and if a generic chair is located in cyberspace, can world builders reference this chair, add their own texture maps, and decorate a house with customized furniture, based on common models? The question nobody seems to be asking is, why do you need a chair in a rendered cyberspace? You can't sit on it, you can only observe it and manipulate it with a mouse.

One quickly comes to realize that the things with the most consistent significance to the intellect are flat. Your office is filled with papers, books and binders. There are file cabinets full of them. There are pictures, posters and charts on the wall. What would be the point of rendering or sculpting them, even if it did not consume a great deal of computer firepower? Digitizing words is easy. When words are digitized, they are stored as text files that can be annotated, referenced and searched. When sounds are digitized, they become audio files that can be replayed, edited, compressed and placed in new contexts. As can video.

Each of these formats is represented by one or more MIME-types. The text, when stored on the Web, has a .txt or .html extension. Audio has .au, .wav, .aiff or .ram. Video is stored as .qt, .mov, .avi, .mpg. And now VRML worlds are stored as .wrl files. Should a World be content? The content handler of a browser has a choice of displaying the World in-line or passing it off to a helper application. When the World is displayed, the only relationship between the parts of the World is spatial. With VRML 2.0 the objects can have behaviors, generate sounds, maintain their state when bumped (rather than passed through) and change through time, but the World is not really a container, any more than an HTML page is. VRML has moved the context handling of Web documents from a hierarchical order to a spayial representation, but did not fundamentally change the relationship of the content to the viewer, reader or browser. The individual interacts with the world. The Worlds and the viewers and the objects do not form binding relationships or interact with one another. Worlds can be probed. Objects manipulated. Responses triggered. But the overall effect is that the viewer is in a robotic suit with tentacles that allow the exploration of an alien terrain.

Executable Content

The VRML browser constitutes a frame, just as the Web browser does. The power of Java is its ability to break out of the frame onto the desktop and draw new windows, each with its own capabilities, context and network connections. While the VRML 2.0 specification is for a descriptive modeling language that specifies light sources, dimensions, relationships and shading, Java is frequently referenced as an example of a programming language to bind to VRML to provide networked communications back to a multiuser server and incorporate advanced behaviors and events within the world. There are already several VRML browsers written in Java. Pundits say that the intersection of VRML and Java will be a significant advance, Java seems to do away with the need for a VRML specification, as the display executables could be delivered with the world, allowing the world builder sole discretion over the modeling language used. The VRML is text that would be read and understood by the Java bytecode, delivered as "application/octet-stream."

`http://www.lab.com/LiveJava/developers/vrml.html`

The incorporation of Java in the VRML 2.0 specification will certainly add some razzledazzle to the formerly static environments. The designers of the VRML 2.0 spec suggest that Java will be the most common language supported by VRML browsers to run scripts. The VRML package includes the following classes and public Java interfaces:

- vrml.Field

  This class defines the display area's nodes and fields that comprise the world. It is descended from Java's Object class by default.

- vrml.Browser

  Allows scripts to get and set browser information, such as name and version using the getName() and getVersion() methods. getCurrentSpeed returns the speed at which the viewpoint is moving. Frame rate is similarly returned. Background and viewpoint have similar binding methods: bindBackground() and bindViewpoint().

- vrml.Script

  While Java is not required as the language to implement logic within environments to determine events based on current variables, such as "if the sun is up AND the vampire is out of his coffin THEN dissolve the vampire."

Context Handler

Let's go back to the chair. In the phenomenal ("real") world, a person's relationship with an object is active, not passive. A chair is to sit. A person sits on the chair. This is Heiddeger's ontological world of activity and utility, as opposed to an ontic world of the "thing in itself." The verb "sit" is tightly bound to the object chair. "Sit" resides in "chair." "Sit," however, also resides on "person." If the world were a computer and you issued the command, "I sit on the chair," you would expect a response of "you are now seated" and/or "the chair squeaks slightly." The verb "sit" resides on the chair as well as on the person. In a computer simulation, if a person tried to sit, the computer would need an order for where to find the verb—on the person, the chair, or on the room.

This brings us to a very different form of virtual reality: the multiuser object-oriented environment, or MOO. It is common in MOO to speak of a verb being "on" an object, or associated with an object, but in fact a MOO-based object is made up of three things, attributes, verbs and properties, much as Java objects are an encapsulation of methods and variables.

- The **attribute** determines an object's genealogy (what verbs and properties it has inherited from its parents) and whether the object is animate or inanimate. If an object is animate, the boolean flag called a player bit is set to 1.

- The **properties** define the object's name (a string, how this object is addressed or invoked), location (which is of the "object" type: what room/container is the object in), the owner (also an object, the player who controls access to the object), contents (a list of objects, what the object is holding, the inverse of "location"). Objects also have several bit properties that relate to powers over other objects and permissions to be affected by other objects.

- The **verb** is a named MOO program that is run when the name is invoked. Verbs cause objects to alter their properties and properties of other objects, much as methods effect change on variables in

Java. For example, "put <object> in <container>" is a common MOO verb that adds an object to the list of objects that make up the "contents" of a container object and alters the location property of the affected object.

In this way, the verb "sit" takes on real meaning in a MOO. If I type "sit" the MOO looks for the verb first on me. If I have defined what I mean by sit, for example, sit Indian-style on the floor, everyone in the room would see "motodave sits Indian style on the floor." Whenever anyone else looked at the room, they would see a list of the rooms contents, and I would appear as "motodave (sitting on the floor indian-style." If I did not have the verb defined, the MOO would look to the room and its contents for the verb. If the verb was not found, the room would "throw an exception," saying, "I don't understand that." If the verb was found on the room, you might be seated in a wicker chair, on a beanbag, or in a movie seat. Other activities and events would be initiated. The lights dims; the curtain opens; the show begins.

The MOO is text-based virtual reality. If you look at the room, you see a description, such as:

```
Makeshift Cafe
The rear of the garden tapers into the tree line. Near a large
forked willow,an open tent shelters a table with various
things used here by the caterers. An area in front of the tent
has tables and chairs for the guests. A lawn table with a few
chairs around it sits unused. Moto is sitting at the bar.
Doug's table sits unused off to the side. An old AM radio plays
progressive post-punk. Someone has left a copy of the newspa-
per lying on the lawn table. An art-deco picturephone labeled
"JAYSHOUSE" rests on the lawn table.
The sun falls rapidly out of sight behind the Los Altos hills.
You see Human Cannon, an RL, the riverside, and a cheap plastic
number puzzle here.
```

There is nobody here now, except for me, the observer. I don't see myself in the scene, unless I sit down.

```
sit
```
You sit down at the lawn table.

```
look
```
Makeshift Cafe
The rear of the garden tapers into the tree line. Near a large
forked willow, an open tent shelters a table with various
things used here by the caterers. An area in front of the tent
has tables and chairs for the guests. **You are sitting at a lawn
table with a closed parasol.** Moto is sitting at the bar. Doug's
table sits unused off to the side. An old AM radio plays pro-
gressive post-punk. Someone has left a copy of the newspaper
lying on the lawn table. An art-deco picturephone labeled
"JAYSHOUSE" rests on the lawn table.

There's no one else around. Moto is not a player, but actually a puppet I left in this room a long time ago and forgot about. I used to hang
out here a few years ago, with a bunch of system administrators and
programmers, talking about bands, shows, dates, books, films, school.
You can look at objects, as well as the room. When you **look** at an
object, the object displays its description and lists its contents and
other properties set by the owner. The "Human Cannon," "RL," "river-
side" and "cheap plastic number puzzle" are other objects someone
left behind.

```
look moto
```
Moto
Just some biker.
He is sleeping.

Look more closely at moto.

```
@examine Moto
```
Moto (#55304) is owned by Suttree (#59696)
Obvious Verbs:
  @follow <anything> with Moto
  @stay Moto
  com*mand Moto to <anything>
  mon*itor Moto
  mon*itor Moto
  ign*ore Moto

```
wh*isper <anything> to Moto
mon(old) Moto
ign(old) Moto
com(old) Moto to <anything>
@gen*der Moto is <anything>
```

Since Moto is my puppet, I can command it to do things like **stay**, **follow** another player, monitor a room I'm not in.

While I'm looking at Moto, Sick comes into the room and sits down. Now, if I looked at the room again, I would see:

Moto and Sick are sitting at the bar.

I look at the Human Cannon and try to put Moto in. The Cannon refuses to accept a nonplayer. I try to fire the cannon but fall in and get blown back to my own room. I'm about to go back and list all the verbs on the cannon. Look at the other objects in the room. Look at myself. Try to build an explanation of how all the objects work together to create a world when I'm interrupted by a page from Spatula, who I haven't seen in ages. "Whatcha been up to?" he asks from across the MOO. I join him in the Hot Tub, where he's soaking with other old friends. Steam billowing up from the tub makes the bright stars twinkle more and the dim stars fade to obscurity. The underwater light is on. The bubbling lights are on. Janus dunks Spatula under the surface for a moment. He comes up spitting.

I am very quickly lost in the shared hallucination, no longer a detached investigator, but a guy hanging out in a Hot Tub with a bunch of freaks.

The Relational Database

The MOO system is a server and a database. The MOO server manages the network connections, maintains queues of commands and tasks to execute, controls access to the database, and executes other MOO code. The database stores representations of all the objects in the MOO, including programmed verbs that give the objects their distinctive behaviors. These "stored procedures" are not unlike the programs or code segments stored in a corporate database application that remind an account representative to call on a delinquent customer 60 days after a bill was due, or the code stored in an Oracle database that generates HTML on the fly when the Web server is hit. Between the server and the database, MOO commands are interpreted. The commands are parsed (read) by the server into a MOO procedure call, or **verb** that does the work of extending or altering the relationships of the data in the database. A MOO is a classic object-relational database that you can see from the inside, as you're a data type.

Access to the MOO is through a terminal interface. A user telnets to a port on the MOO server and logs in. All activity happens on the server, with the user having a character-only display. Without the visual cues of a GUI interface, the MOO can become confusing. There are many commands to remember, which cannot be presented in buttons, menus and other controls. The layout can become confusing as users dig new areas and the terrain sprawls. How do I get from the Living Room to the Hot Tub? I look at the room I'm in and see the exits. I remember that the Hot Tub is out in the garden, so I go south and wind up on the Deck, then descend the stairs into the Hot Tub. That wasn't so hard, because they were only a few rooms apart. Finding other areas requires traversing vast gardens, climbing mountains, entering caves, spelunking, encountering subterranean rivers, paying the boatman, then following a map to your destination. You could have simply teleported yourself there, but you would have to remember the object number, as the command "go Hades" will return an exception ("There's no such place known") as the database entry is not accessible, or joined, to the room from which the query is made. You would have typed "go #11273" to get to Hades or would have had to add the room to a list that is stored with your other contents on your persona.

You find yourself facing the same problems in a text-based MOO as you encountered in VRML. You realize that you need a magic lantern to transport you where you need to go. The magic lantern must be aware of the objects in this world and throughout cyberspace. It must be right at hand, on the desktop, yet able to query a vast database, pull the information together into a report, then act on information. Cyberspace is now beginning to sound like the database frontends, protocols and connectivity we discussed in the last chapter, but with a twist. The users that are querying the database are also communicating with each other. On a level that is still abstract, we are bridging the fundamental dichotomies of the Internet.

An important distinction begins to emerge between the two types of virtual reality we have been discussing.

TABLE 3.

	MOO	VRML
Distribution	Server-based	Client-based
Protocol	Login with Telnet	Download with HTTP
Component	Database	Interface
Purpose	Real-time communications	Publishing and presentation of information
Data type	Text	Model

The differences between the two types of virtual reality offer another opportunity to explore the major distinctions between applications for presenting information to an audience over time (publishing) and applications for sharing information between users in realtime or over a short time (communication). The applications are bound by their protocols: MOO uses Telnet to tie users together through socket connections to write to each other's screens with an immediacy that creates a sense of space through the display and manipulation of words through time. VRML uses HTTP to transfer the World to the desktop, then for hyperlinking objects within the world to files located around the Internet.

The designers of VRML claim the first VRML browser was built not so much to display a world model, but to demonstrate the efficacy of the Cyberspace Protocol, which would break up VRML worlds into their constituent parts, located on physically disparate servers. The Cyberspace Protocol would enable browsers to query multiple worlds and dynamically render the borders of perception. The thinking was, with a fixed, three-dimensional cyberspace, it was predetermined what was next to you, coming up, behind you if you turned around. The Cyberspace Protocol was based on the continuity of space and was an attempt to impose that rigid structure on an essentially anarchic, dynamic and fluid medium.

Returning to the thought of our first chapter, we remember how the Web paved the Net, with one monolithic protocol defining the relationships and structure of the perceived network. VRML and the concept of the Cyberspace Protocol attempt a unification of cyberspace, trapping the observer in an ever more determinate system. It is less about visualization, imagination or interaction than it is a reification of the old order in the new. It is reminiscent of the Wyndam Lewis/ James Joyce arguments that resulted in Joyce's characterization of Lewis in *Finnegans Wake* as a "spacialist," affirming Space at the expense of time. Sight over sound. Looking over listening. Watching over participating. Weight over levity. Publications over communications.

If you subscribe to the VRML list, you read constant battles about standards and directions, architecture, scripting languages, descriptive formats. Similarly, on the WWW working group list there are arguments against innovations that improve capabilities at the expense of legacy content. At the birth of the Web, there was dissatisfaction and name calling on the part of those who had invested time and resources in Gopher services. A theoretically "open" system such as the Internet was, until Java, rapidly losing its ability to innovate under the weight of a sudden critical mass of users and the investments of that audience. What had been a dictatorship of standards bodies and architecture groups suddenly became a dictatorship of the market. The content producer had to follow or lose the audience.

Java: The Bomb-throwing Anarchist

Rather than agreeing on standards, Java allows us to write our own and deploy them on the micro level. We do not need to abide by data formats, markup languages, communications protocols, or rendering libraries. To prove this point, we will decide how we want to interact, what we want to share, how we want to appear, and how we want our environment presented. We will choose the Internet services that best suit our needs and build on those. The Internet already has many applications and protocols, each of which fills an important niche. We will integrate them into our own functioning cyberspace that so that we can invite our friends, order pizza, get some work done, or just hang out.

To prove our point, we will design our own protocol, the Cyberspace Communications Protocol (CCP), our own descriptive language, the Real-Time Markup Language (RTML), write our own suite of applications, the **MoonBean** package to demonstrate its efficacy.

```
http://www.lab.com/LiveJava/developers/moonbean.html
```

CHAPTER 24   *Socket to Cyberspace*

Currently, we have two mechanisms for communicating online: an immersive, interactive MOO and a static web. The idea behind Moon-Bean was to connect the two, so we could become immersed in the web and use it as part of an interactive communication space.

Before it could be determined how MoonBean would work, we had to decide what MoonBean was supposed to do. Basically, MoonBean must open and maintain a connection (socket) to the MOO, much like a Telnet application. MoonBean must also provide a graphical user interface (GUI), allowing the user to interact with the MOO. Finally, MoonBean must be able to display documents in the Web browser and simultaneously convey state information to the Telnet window and other GUI elements.

Because we are striving for multiple-party, extended communications, HTTP will not do. Because we want to share audio and video files, look at graphic representations of objects, Telnet will not do. We want to manipulate a database in real time. We want to reach out into cyberspace. The only way to achieve this is to have all the participants open a socket connection from their client computer to a server and pass signals over that channel that effect changes the database, which passes new state information along socket connections to the other players, enacting events on their desktops. A socket is nothing more than a connection between two things, in this case between the MoonBean client and the MOO server.

Cyberspace Communications Protocol (CCP)

Defining a socket in Java is pretty easy, since the standard API already has socket objects built in. Simply import the Socket class, and create an instance of the Socket. The "instance object of the Socket class needs to connect somewhere. To do that, we need this code snippet somewhere (such as the init() method) in the class we are creating:

```
socket = new Socket("butterfly.net", 8888);
```

This actually creates a new instance of the Socket class, connected to the specified host and port. The new instance replaces the old, unconnected instance.

Anyway, the socket is now connected. At least, we hope so. What happens if the socket doesn't connect? It will throw an exception. In fact, Java will not compile your class unless you watch for these exceptions. The Socket constructor above may throw an Unknown-HostException if the host is not found, or an IOException in case there is an IO problem. To catch these exceptions, we write the code like this:

```
import java.applet.Applet;
import java.net.Socket;

public class SocketDemo extends Applet {
  Socket socket;
```

```
. . .

    }
```

The code inside the catch clause will be run only in the event that an exception is thrown by the Socket constructor. Here, we only display the error. An alternative solution would be to cause the applet to exit, or prompt the user for a new host and port, and try again.

If this succeeds, we now have a connected socket. But that's no good if we can't read from and write to the socket. To do this, the socket has two streams associated with it, an InputStream and an Output-Stream. A Stream is defined abstractly as a flow of data. In our case, we're interested in the flow of text into and out of the socket. To use the streams, we have to 'get' them from the socket.

However, Streams come in many flavors, and the Java library defines a bunch of them for us. For our socket, we need to read and write entire lines of text at once. Also, anything sent to the socket's Output-Stream should be sent immediately, and not buffered inside the stream, if this is to be interactive.

For the input stream, Michael Reece, the programmer, chose a DataInputStream. According to the Java API, this stream will allow me to read one line of text at a time.

For the output stream, he chose a PrintStream. This stream allows him to write one line of text at a time. And, while it is not using it for printing, it can still take advantage of its "auto-flush" feature, so text sent out to the socket will not be buffered.

For our class, we now have three instance variables:

```
Socket socket;
DataInputStream inStream;
PrintStream outStream;
```

The sockets now exist, but are still not connected to the socket. To do this, we change the initialization code to:

```
try {
   socket = new Socket("butterfly.net", 7777);
   inStream = new DataInputStream(
     new BufferedInputStream(socket.getInputStream()));
   outStream = new PrintStream(
     new BufferedOutputStream(socket.getOutputStream()),
                  true);
} catch (Exception e) {
   System.out.println("Exception opening socket: " + e);
}
```

The important thing to notice here is the call to socket.getInput-Stream() and socket.getOutputStream(). The way streams are constructed is a little tricky. Let's take a look at this line:

```
inStream = new DataInputStream(
        new BufferedInputStream(socket.getInputStream()));
```

If you read this from end to front, here's what's happening. First, get the input stream from the socket. Next, connect that to a BufferedIn-putStream, so that any data coming in from the socket will be buffered until we are ready to use it. Then, connect that to a DataInputStream, which allows us to read arbitrary values (particularly, lines of text!) from the stream. Finally, assign this newly constructed stream to the inStream instance we created.

Something similar happens in the next statement:

```
outStream = new PrintStream(
   new BufferedOutputStream(socket.getOutputStream()),
        true);
```

First, we get the output stream from the socket and connect it to a BufferedOutputStream, so that anything we send to the socket will be buffered until the socket is ready to handle it. Next, connect this to a PrintStream, so we can take advantage of its auto-flush feature, and force the socket to read everything from the buffer every time we write anything to it. If you look closely, the "true" argument is actually the second parameter of the PrintStream constructor and means "yes, use auto-flush for this PrintStream." This is all defined in the Java API.

Now, whenever we need to read from the socket, we can do this:

aString = inStream.readLine();

And to write to the socket, we can use:

outStream.println(aString);

When the socket is disconnected, the readLine method above will return 'null'. We can put this fact to good use and keep reading from the socket until it is disconnected (in a Thread's run() method, for example).

```
String incoming;
try {
    while ((incoming = inStream.readLine()) != null) {
    // do something with incoming text
  }
  } catch (IOException e) {
  System.out.println("Socket is no longer connected.");
  }
```

Now that we see how sockets work, we can use these in any applet.

Graphic User Interface

The next step was to create an interface for the user. This consists primarily of a window (Frame) outside the browser that contains a TextArea, where incoming text will be displayed, and a TextField, for the user to type in.

For this, we need more instance objects.

```
Frame window;
TextArea display;
TextField user;
```

These AWT objects would then be constructed and displayed according to the API. Since all of these pieces are working together, it's best to encapsulate them into a single object. And, since all of this will be interacting with the socket, we'll encapsulate that as well. To do this, we need to create a new class, which will be derived from Frame.

```
  class SocketFrame extends Frame {
    Socket socket;
 DataInputStream inStream;
   PrintStream outStream;
     TextArea display;
   TextField user;
     . . .
}
```

This class will need a constructor, so it can be instantiated. All the constructor needs to do is call its inherited constructor.

```
    public SocketFrame() {        super();      }
```

Now that we have our TextArea (display) and TextField (user), let's do something with them. First, we need to initialize them. So, we add a new method to our SocketFrame to do this work.

```
  public void setupGUI() {
   user = new TextField(80);
  this.add("South", user);
 display = new TextArea(20, 80);
    this.add("North", display);
  this.resize(500, 400);
this.show();        }
```

Here, we create a new TextField, which we intend to hold 80 characters, and add that to the "southern" end of the frame. Next, a 20 by 80 TextArea is created and added to the "northern" end. The last two lines merely resize the frame and show it on the screen.

Next, let's create a method to do similar initializations on the socket.

```
public boolean setupSocket() {
   try {
     socket = new Socket("butterfly.net", 7777);
     inStream = new DataInputStream(
               new BufferedInputStream(socket.getInput
                 Stream()));
     outStream = new PrintStream(
               new BufferedOutputStream(socket.getOut
                 putStream()),
                 true);
   } catch (Exception e) {
     System.out.println("Exception opening socket: " + e);
     return false;
   }
   return true;
}
```

This code should look familiar. The only thing new is this method returns a boolean (true or false) value. It will return "false" if there is an exception and "true" if everything goes as planned. This provides an easy way for another object to call this method and see if it succeeded.

Finally, we need to pay attention to the user TextField and see when the Enter key is pressed. When this event happens, we'll echo the text to the display TextArea, send it to the output stream, and clear the field for the new input.

```
public boolean keyDown(Event e, int key) {
    if (e.target == user && key == 10) {
      String s = user.getText();
      display.appendText("> " + s + "\n");
      user.setText("");
      if (outStream != null) outStream.println(s);
      return true;
    }
    return false;
}
```

The keyDown() method is part of the AWT and will be called automatically when a key is pressed inside our frame. The event-handling methods of the AWT are designed to return "true" if the event was intercepted and acted on and false otherwise.

MOO 'n' Java = MoonBean

Now, we have a working socket and GUI. All that's left is to create an applet that puts our hard work to use.

```
public class SocketDemo extends Applet implements Runnable {
  SocketFrame window;      Thread thread;
    . . .
}
```

Notice that we are implementing the Runnable interface and have created a Thread instance within the applet. Multithreaded programming is a key feature of Java, and we might as well put it to work for us.

The Runnable interface says that our class will define a run() method. This is necessary so the Thread can be 'attached' to our applet. You'll see this more below.

But first, let's initialize our applet. All applets have an init() method that is called automatically. Here's ours:

```
public void init() {
  window = new SocketFrame();
  window.setupGUI();
  window.display.appendText("* Connecting...\n");
  if (window.setupSocket())
    window.display.appendText("* Connected!\n");
  else {
    window.display.appendText("* NOT connected!\n");
    window.socket = null;
  }
}
```

First, we construct a new SocketFrame (which we created above) and assign it to our "window" instance. Then, call the window's set-upGUI() method, defined above, to get the GUI ready. We can also reference the window's "display" instance and append text to it from here.

Next, we call the window's setupSocket() method, doing one thing if it returns "true" and another if it fails.

Every applet also has a start() method that is called when the applet is started. This is a good place to set up our thread.

```
 public void start() {
if (thread == null) {
 thread = new Thread(this);
 thread.start();
  }
}
```

The thread will begin its life as a "null" object. After making sure it is in this state, we construct a new Thread, attached to our applet (this). Check the API for a better understanding of this Thread constructor. All that's left is to "start" the thread. Doing so will call the run() method on our applet. This is why we declared that the applet "implements Runnable." The thread knows it can call the applet's run() method.

```
public void run() {
   String incoming;
   try {
     while ((incoming = window.inStream.readLine()) != null)
        window.display.appendText(incoming + "\n");
   } catch (Exception e) {
     System.out.println("* Exception: " + e);
     window.socket = null;
   }
}
```

This run() method will continue to execute the while loop until there is an exception (the socket is disconnected), or until the thread is stopped. Which leads to the final method for our applet.

```
public void stop() {
  if ((thread != null) && (window.socket == null)) {
    thread.stop();
  thread = null;
  }
}
```

An applet's stop() method will be called when you leave the Web page that contained the applet. Here, we first make sure the thread is running (is not "null") and make sure the socket is not still connected (is "null"). The last part is necessary if we do not want the thread to stop just because we go to a new location in the browser when we're still connected to the socket.

After making sure it is ok to do so, we call the thread's stop() method, which will terminate the applet's run() method, assuming run() is still going. In our case, run() will be completed (and socket will = "null") before our thread is ever stopped, but it's still a good idea to stop the thread anyway.

At this stage, we have an applet that will connect to the MOO, display incoming text from the MOO, and accept user input to send text back to the MOO.

Satellites

All this is accomplished with very little code and demonstrates the power of Java.

Here is the finished result, SocketDemo.java:

```
import java.applet.*;
import java.awt.*;
import java.net.*;
import java.io.*;

public class SocketDemo extends Applet implements Runnable {

    SocketFrame window;
    Thread thread;

    public void init() {
      window = new SocketFrame();
      window.setupGUI();
      window.display.appendText("* Connecting...\n");
      if (window.setupSocket())
        window.display.appendText("* Connected!\n");
      else {
        window.display.appendText("* NOT connected!\n");
        window.socket = null;
      }
    }

    public void run() {
      String incoming;
      try {
```

```java
      while ((incoming = window.inStream.readLine()) != null)
         window.display.appendText(incoming + "\n");
      } catch (Exception e) {
        System.out.println("* Exception: " + e);
        window.socket = null;
      }
    }

    public void start() {
      if (thread == null) {
        thread = new Thread(this);
        thread.start();
      }
    }

    public void stop() {
      if ((thread != null) && (window.socket == null)) {
        thread.stop();
        thread = null;
      }
    }
  }

class SocketFrame extends Frame {
  Socket socket;
  DataInputStream inStream;
  PrintStream outStream;

  TextArea display;
  TextField user;

  public SocketFrame() {
    super();
  }

  public void setupGUI() {
    user = new TextField(80);
    this.add("South", user);
    display = new TextArea(20, 80);
    this.add("North", display);
    this.resize(500, 400);
    this.show();
  }
```

```
public boolean setupSocket() {
  try {
    socket = new Socket("butterfly.net", 7777);
    inStream = new DataInputStream(
      new BufferedInputStream(socket.getInputStream()));
    outStream = new PrintStream(
      new BufferedOutputStream(socket.getOutputStream()),
      true);
  } catch (Exception e) {
    System.out.println("Exception opening socket: " + e);
    return false;
  }
  return true;
}

public boolean keyDown(Event e, int key) {
  if (e.target == user && key == 10) {
    String s = user.getText();
    display.appendText("> " + s + "\n");
    user.setText("");
    if (outStream != null) outStream.println(s);
    return true;
  }
  return false;
}

}
```

All that's left is to create an web page to contain the applet. Here's socketdemo.html:

```
<html>
<head>    <title>Socket demo</title>    </head>
<body>    SocketDemo applet
  <hr>
  <applet
  code="SocketDemo.class" width=100 height=100>    </applet>
  </body>
</html>
```

And that's it!

Real-Time Markup Language (RTML)

What's left for MoonBean? The rest of MoonBean's job is to pay attention to incoming text, and check to see if it is a "MoonBean protocol message." If so, it must parse the message and do something special, such as display a web page in the browser. To do this, we have to hook onto the browser, using the applet's getAppletContext() method. We can then call the context's showDocument() method, like so:

```
getAppletContext().showDocument(someURL);
```

Listening for and acting on these messages is the real core to Moon-Bean and a tad more difficult than the SocketDemo class above. But what you have so far is a good guide to beginning your own projects in Java and some insight into how we've approached ours.

The MoonBean Parser

What makes MoonBean more than a Telnet client is its ability to play audio and display graphics or Web documents. MoonBean does this in cooperation with the MOO through a minimal protocol.

Every time a line of text is read from the socket, it is checked to see if it is a 'MoonBean protocol message'. If so, it must parse the message and do something special; all other text is simply displayed to the user.

When a connection is first established, the MOO sends the message:

```
@#MoonBean version 1.0
```

MoonBean will ignore any other protocol messages until it receives this message. Only after parsing has been enabled, will it respond to other messages. Handshaking continues when the MOO sends:

```
@#MoonBean login
```

This opens MoonBean's login dialog, accepting a user name and password for connecting to the MOO. The name and password are sent back to the MOO for verification. If the login is not successful, the MOO resends the login command, and this cycle continues until a valid name and password are given. Upon success, the MOO sends:

```
@#MoonBean connected
```

MoonBean will respond to this with:

```
@#MoonBean secure-key <key>
```

This command is the only protocol message that is sent *by* MoonBean (all others are sent *to* MoonBean). Without receiving this, the MOO continues to behave traditionally, allowing regular text-based connections via telnet.

When the MOO receives this command, it establishes that the client is capable of handling further protocol messages, and will enable its enhancements for displaying web documents, etc, to the user. The MOO also notes the <key> sent by the client, which is generated randomly by MoonBean for each connection. From this point on, MoonBean will ignore any further messages that do not contain this key.

This prevents malicious MOO programmers from "spoofing" MoonBean by bypassing $bean_utils, which has its own security restrictions for allowing access by approved programmers. All further messages will be sent in the form:

```
@#MoonBean <key> <request>
```

Acceptable requests are:

```
display-url <url>
```

MoonBean will display the given URL in the browser.

```
audio-play <url>
```

MoonBean will play the audio clip specified by the gievn URL.

```
audio-loop <url>   [Not yet implemented]
```

MoonBean begins looping the specified audio clipc.

```
audio-stop <url>   [Not yet implemented]
```

If MoonBean is looping the specified audio clip, it is stopped.

```
tool-add <label> <command>
```

Adds a new button to the floating toolbar with the specified label. Clicking the button sends the command back to the moo. If the toolbar does not yet exist, it is created.

```
tool-remove <label>
```

Removes the specified button from the toolbar. If no more buttons exist, the toolbar is removed from the screen.

```
menu-define <menu> [ <item>:<cmd> | $<sub-menu>$ ] ...
```

Creates a new menu labeled <menu> or replaces an existing one. Further parameters are optional, and if they exist will add items to the new menu. Each parameter can be one of:

```
<item>:<cmd>
```

A menu item labeled <item> which, when selected, will send <cmd> to the MOO. If no <cmd> is given, a disabled item is added. If <item> is "-", a menu seperator line is added. $<sub-menu>$

A nested menu, labeled <sub-menu>. Items can be added to the sub-menu using menu-additem message below.

```
menu-additem <menu> <item>:<cmd> | $<sub-menu>$ ...
```

Adds items to the specified menu if it exists. The <menu> can be a top-level menu, or a nested menu. Each parameter can be a item and command pair or a nested sub-menu, as with the menu-define parameters above.

```
menu-rmitem <menu> <item> ...
```

Removes items from the specified menu (or sub-menu). Each <item> can be a menu item label or nested sub-menu label. Note that with the menu-rmitem message, sub-menu labels are not delimited with $'s.

```
menu-destroy <menu>
```

Removes the top-level or nested menu labelled <menu>.

```
send-back <command>
```

Send the given command back to the MOO as typed by the user. This can be particularly dangerous (to a MOO character, not their computer) and should be closely guarded, preferably only accessible by MOO wizards.

Any parameter that is more than one word should be contained in "quotation marks" for proper parsing by MoonBean. Here is a typical example:

```
@#MoonBean 24134213 tool-add "what's new" "read
  newspaper"
```

## CHAPTER 25

The MoonBean Package

Guide to the Java Source

MoonBean is made up of several Java classes and MOO objects. The Java classes are defined in the following source files which are part of the husky.mb package:

- MoonBean.java (MoonBean.class)

  The MoonBean applet, controls the execution thread responsible for reading from the socket.

- MBWindow.java (MBWindow.class)

  Contains the GUI interface, socket, and streams.

- MBParser.java (MBParser.class)

  The MoonBean protocol parser, responsible for detecting and parsing protocol messages.

- MBTextArea.java (MBTextArea.class)

  An improved TextArea class, used by MBWindow for displaying text. It enhances java.awt.TextArea by providing line wrapping and scrollback trimming.

- MBLoginDialog.java (MBLoginDialog.class)

  The login dialog, invoked by the parser.

- MBToolbar.java (MBToolbar.class and MBTool.class)

  The toolbar and tool button classes. A MBTool object is an enhanced java.awt.Button that contains a MOO command attached to the button. A MBToolbar object is a Frame that contains multiple MBTool objects, and sends commands to the socket in response to button presses.

- MBMenuBar.java (MBMenuBar.class and MBMenuItem.java)

  The menubar and item classes. A MBMenuItem object is an enhanced java.awt.MenuItem that contains a MOO command. MBMenuBar is a complex MenuBar that contains MBMenuItems. MBMenuBar is also responsible for parsing much of the menu related MoonBean syntax, and knows how to create, locate and replace, and remove menus and items.

- Words.java (Words.class)

  The Words class facilitates string parsing by matching "quoted word groups" and treating them as a single word. This object is more general in purpose, and is not part of the husky.mb package. Instead, it is contained in the husky.util package.

Related MOO Code

- MoonBean utilities ($bean_utils)

  Contains the programmer interface for sending MoonBean protocol messages to the user. See the seperate section on $bean_utils for more information on using the MoonBean utilities object in your MOO code.

- MoonBean menu utilities ($menu_utils)

Contains the programmer interface for creating and updating a standard set of menus for exploring and manipulating MOO objects. This object is not a requirement for MoonBean, and will generally be unique for every MOO. For these reasons, it will not be covered in detail.

MoonBean.java

```
/*
 * @(#)MoonBean.java1.0  06/07/96  sick@butterfly.net
 *
 * Copyright (c) 1996 HuskyLabs, Inc. All rights reserved.
 *
 */


/*
```

MoonBean.java contains the MoonBean applet class, the primary part of the MoonBean package. Compiling the applet:

Source .java files should be in a directory classes/husky/mb/.

They should be compiled from the classes/ directory with:

javac husky/mb/MoonBean.java etc.

Using the applet on the web:

Compiled .class files should be in a directory ./classes/ husky/mb/ beneath the web page.

The MoonBean applet accepts the following optional parameters:

Host	The host to connect to (ex, butterfly.net) default is the .html document base. While other values are allowed, Netscape will generally throw a socket security exception. If the moo is running on the same machine as the web server, it is generally best to omit this parameter.
Port	The port to connect to (ex, 8888) default is 8888. If the moo is listening on a different port, provide this parameter.
Target	The browser frame for displaying MB related URLs (ex, MBTarget) default is MBTarget.

Sample .html file for this applet:

```
<html>

<head> <title>MoonBean demo</title> </head>

<body>

<h2>MoonBean demo</h2><hr>

<applet code="husky/mb/MoonBean.class" cod
 base="classes"

 width=45 height=45>

<param name="port" value="7777">

</applet>

</body>
```

```
     </html>

*/


package husky.mb;  // MoonBean is part of the husky.mb package


import java.applet.Applet;    // for the Applet class
import java.io.IOException;   // for socket/stream exceptions
import java.awt.Graphics;     // for painting connection status
import java.awt.Color;


/**
 * MoonBean is a client applet for a MOO server capable of
 *    displaying web-
 * based multimedia content in an interactive environment.
 */
public class MoonBean extends Applet implements Runnable {

  // these are static so they are the same across all instances
  //    of the
  // applet, public so other objects may reference them, and
  //    final so
  // subclasses cannot override them.

  /**
   * the name of this product
   */
  public static final String productName = "MoonBean";

  /**
   * the current version number
   */
  public static final String productVers = "1.0";

  /**
   * whether debugging info will be displayed to the console
   */
  final boolean DEBUG = true;
```

```java
Thread theThread;   // controls the applet
MBWindow window;    // the user interface window; contains
// socket & streams
MBParser parser;    // MoonBean protocol parser

String host;        // host to connect to, passed as <PARAM>
int port;           // port to connect to, passed as <PARAM>
String target;      // frame for browsing, passes as <PARAM>
//
// inherited methods
//


/**
 * initializes MoonBean by getting host, port, and target
 *   parameters, and
 * setting up the GUI.
 */
public void init() {
  String s;
  s = getParameter("host");
  host = (s != null) ? s : getDocumentBase().getHost();
  s = getParameter("port");
  port = (s != null) ? Integer.parseInt(s) : 8888;
  s = getParameter("target");
  target = (s != null) ? s : "MBTarget";
}


/**
 * start or resume the applet and thread
 */
public void start() {
  showDebug("entering start()");
  if (theThread == null) {
    showDebug("starting thread");
    theThread = new Thread(this);
    theThread.start();
  }
}
```

```
/**
 * runs the thread.
 * sets up the GUI and socket, and loops until the socket is
 *    closed.
 */
public void run() {
  showDebug("entering run()");

  // set up the telnet window
  window = new MBWindow(this);
  window.show();

  // set up the parser, passing it this, the target frame,
  //    and the menu bar
  parser = new MBParser(this, target, window.mb);

  // if socket is not connected, try to connect
  if (window.socket == null) {
    window.display.appendTextln("* Connecting to " + host +
      ":" + port + "...");
    if (window.setupSocket(host, port)) {
      window.display.appendTextln("* Connected!");
    } else {
      window.display.appendTextln("* Unable to connect to "
        + host + ".");
      return;  // abort
    }
  }


  repaint();  // repaint the applet to show connection status

  String incoming;  // one line of text from the socket
  try {
    // this is the main loop for the thread. this loop will
    //    end when the
    // socket is closed and .readLine() returns null.
    while ((incoming = window.istream.readLine()) != null) {
```

```
                // see if incoming is a MoonBean protocol message
                if (parser.isMessage(incoming)) {
                  parser.parseMessage(incoming);
                } else {
                  window.display.appendTextln(incoming);
                }
              }
            } catch (IOException e) {
              System.out.println("* IOException in run() => " + e);
            } finally {
              window.display.appendTextln("* Connection closed.");
              window.socket = null;

              repaint();   // repaint the applet to show connection
            // status

              showDebug("exiting run()");
            }
          }


          /**
           * stop or suspend the applet and thread. the thread is
           *    stopped only if
           * the socket is not connected.
           */
          public void stop() {
            showDebug("entering stop()");
            // do not stop thread while socket is connected
            if ((theThread != null) && (window == null || window.socket
              == null)) {
              showDebug("stopping thread");
              theThread.stop();
              theThread = null;
            }
          }


          /**
           * return information about the parameters this applet
           *    accepts.
           */
```

```
public String[][] getParameterInfo() {
  String pinfo[][] = {
    {"host", "address", "the address to connect to"},
    {"port", "integer", "the port to connect to"},
    {"target", "string", "target frame for browsing"}
  };
  return pinfo;
}


/**
 * return information about this applet.
 */
public String getAppletInfo() {
  return (productName + " " + productVers + "\n" +
    "Copyright (c) 1996 HuskyLabs, Inc.\n" +
    "Programmer, Michael Reece (sick@butterfly.net)");
}


/**
 * called then the applet is painted.
 * override to display connection status.
 * @param g the Graphics object for this applet
 */
public void paint(Graphics g) {

  // display status as a red octagon (if not connected) or a
  //    green circle
  // (if connected)
  if ((window == null) || (window.socket == null)) {
    // x and y points for the octagon
    int[] xs = {15, 30, 40, 40, 30, 15,  5,  5, 15};
    int[] ys = { 5,  5, 15, 30, 40, 40, 30, 15, 5};
    g.setColor(Color.red);
    g.fillPolygon(xs, ys, 9);
    g.setColor(Color.white);
    g.drawString("OFF", 12, 28);
  } else {
    g.setColor(new Color(0,128,0));
    g.fillOval(5, 5, 35, 35);
    g.setColor(Color.white);
    g.drawString("ON", 15, 28);
```

```
        }

    }


    //
    // new methods
    //


    /**
     * Display a debugging string to the console.
     * @param s the string to be displayed
     */
    void showDebug(String s) {
      if (this.DEBUG) System.out.println("MoonBean: " + s);
    }


} // class MoonBean


// end of file MoonBean.java, sick@butterfly.net
```

MBWindow.java

```
 * @(#)MBToolbar.java  1.0  06/07/96  sick@butterfly.net
 *
 * Copyright (c) 1996 HuskyLabs, Inc. All rights reserved.
 *
 */

/*

MBToolbar.java contains the MBToolbar and MBTool classes.
MBToolbar is a frame that contains multiple MBTool objects.
MBTool is a Button with a moo command attached.

*/
```

```
package husky.mb;


import java.awt.Button;        // GUI classes
import java.awt.Event;
import java.awt.Frame;
import java.awt.GridLayout;
import java.util.Vector;        // vector for tools


/**
 * the toolbar frame.
 */
class MBToolbar extends Frame {

  MBParser parent;   // the parser controlling this toolbar


  //
  // constructors
  //


  /**
   * constructor
   *
   * @param parser the MBParser controlling this toolbar
   * @param tools  the tools vector to be placed in the toolbar
   */
  public MBToolbar(MBParser parser, Vector tools) {
    super("Tools");

    this.parent = parser;

    updateWith(tools);
  }


  //
  // inherited methods
  //
```

```java
/**
 * action method; responds to tool button pushes by sending
 * its attached moo command.
 */
public boolean action(Event e, Object arg) {
  String label = (String)arg;

  if (e.target instanceof MBTool) {
    parent.showDebug("toolbar push: " + arg);
    parent.doSendCommand(((MBTool)e.target).command);
  }

  return false;
}


//
// new methods
//


/**
 * updates the toolbar with a new tools vector
 *
 * @param tools the new tools vector
 */
public void updateWith(Vector tools) {
  int tnum = tools.size();

  int cols = 1;
  int rows = tnum;

  removeAll();

  setLayout(new GridLayout(rows, cols));
  for (int i=0; i < tnum; i ++) {
    add((MBTool)tools.elementAt(i));
  }
  pack();
}


} // class MBToolbar
```

```
/**
 * a tool that fits in the toolbar. a MBTool is a Button with
 *    a moo command
 * attached.
 */
class MBTool extends Button {

  String command;  // the moo command


  //
  // constructors
  //


  /**
    * constructor
    *
    * @param label the label for this tool button
    * @param cmd    the moo command for this tool
    */
  public MBTool(String label, String cmd) {
    super(label);
    command = cmd;
  }


} // class MBTool


// end of file MBToolbar.java, sick@butterfly.net
```

MBParser.java

```
/*
 * @(#)MBParser.java1.0  06/07/96  sick@butterfly.net
 *
 * Copyright (c) 1996 HuskyLabs, Inc. All rights reserved.
 *
```

```
    */

    /*

    MPParser takes care of parsing MoonBean protocol messages.
    Messages follow this format:

      @#MoonBean [<key>] <command ...>
```

Some <command> tokens include arguments. See the token definitions in the class for general command formats.

The parser ignores all messages until it receives the ENABLE command: @#MoonBean version <ver>

The <key> token is not used until the parser receives the CONNECT command: @#MoonBean connected

When CONNECT is received, MoonBean should respond with the SENDKEY command: @#MoonBean secure-key <key>

All subsequent messages will be expected to include that <key>. Any that do not are ignored.

See the token definitions below, and the protocol.txt file for more details.

```
    */



    package husky.mb;


    import husky.util.Words;    // for "words" parsing
    import java.util.Vector;    // toolbar vector
    import java.net.URL;        // network classes
    import java.net.MalformedURLException;
```

```java
/**
 * the MoonBean protocol parser.
 */
class MBParser {

  // protocol tokens
  final String ATTN     = "@#MoonBean";   // header
  final String ENABLE   = "version";      // version <ver>
  final String LOGIN    = "login";        // login
  final String CONNECT  = "connected";    // connected
  final String BROWSE   = "display-url";  // display-url <url>
  final String AUPLAY   = "audio-play";   // audio-play <url>
  final String AULOOP   = "audio-loop";   // audio-loop <url>
  final String AUSTOP   = "audio-stop";   // audio-stop <url>
  final String ADDTOOL  = "tool-add";     // tool-add <label>
  // <command> ...
  final String RMTOOL   = "tool-remove";  // tool-remove
  // <label>
  final String SENDBACK = "send-back";    // send-back
  // <command> ...
  final String DEFMENU  = "menu-define";  // menu-define <menu>
  // [<item:cmd> | $<sub>$ ... ]
  final String MENUADD  = "menu-additem"; // menu-add <menu>
  // <item:cmd> | $<sub>$ ...
  final String MENURM   = "menu-rmitem";  // menu-remove <menu>
  // <item> ...
  final String KILLMENU = "menu-destroy"; // menu-destroy
  // <menu>

  final String SENDKEY  = "secure-key";   // secure-key <key>

  MoonBean mbApplet;          // hook to MoonBean
  String mbTarget;            // name of browser frame to show
  // documents
  MBMenuBar mbMenuBar;        // hook to MoonBean.window.mb

  boolean isEnabled = false;  // other tokens ignored until
  // ENABLE received
  String sessionKey = null;   // no secure key until CONNECT
  // received

  Vector tools = new Vector();
```

```
MBToolbar toolbar = null;

//
// constructors
//


/**
 * constructor
 *
 * @param applet hook to the MoonBean applet containing this
 *    instance
 * @param target the target frame for displaying URLs
 * @param mb      the menu bar attached to the applet's
 *    MBWindow
 */
public MBParser(MoonBean applet, String target, MBMenuBar
  mb) {
  this.mbApplet = applet;
  this.mbTarget = target;
  this.mbMenuBar = mb;
}


//
// new methods
//


/**
 * is message a MoonBean protocol message?
 *
 * @returns true iff message starts with ATTN token
 */
public boolean isMessage(String message) {
  return message.startsWith(ATTN);
}


/**
 * parses the protocol message and does any necessary action
 *
```

```
 * @param message the protocol message
 */
public void parseMessage(String message) {
  showDebug("parsing '" + message + "'");

  Words words = new Words(message);
  String key = "";
  String cmd = "";
  String arg = "";

  if (!words.nextWord().equals(ATTN)) {
    showDebug("expected " + ATTN);
    return;
  }
  if (sessionKey != null) {
    key = words.nextWord();
    if (key == null || !key.equals(this.sessionKey)) {
      showDebug("expected key");
      return;
    }
  }
  if ((cmd = words.nextWord()) == null) {
    showDebug("expected command, out of words");
    return;
  }
  arg = words.remainingWords();
  showDebug("key = " + key + "; cmd = " + cmd + "; arg = '"
    + arg + "'");

  if (!this.isEnabled) {
    if (cmd.equals(ENABLE)) {
      showDebug("enabling");
      this.isEnabled = true;
    } else {
      showDebug("not yet enabled");
    }
    return;
  }

  if (cmd.equals(ENABLE))showDebug("already enabled");
  else if (cmd.equals(LOGIN))    doLogin();
  else if (cmd.equals(CONNECT)) {
    if (this.sessionKey == null) {
```

```
            this.sessionKey = generateKey();
            doSendCommand(ATTN + " " + SENDKEY + " " +
               this.sessionKey, false);
         } else {
           showDebug("requested new key?! sessionKey=" +
             this.sessionKey);
         }
     } else if (cmd.equals(BROWSE))   doBrowse(arg);
     else if (cmd.equals(AUPLAY))     doPlayAudio(arg);
     else if (cmd.equals(AULOOP))     doLoopAudio(arg);
     else if (cmd.equals(AUSTOP))     doStopLoop(arg);
     else if (cmd.equals(ADDTOOL))    doAddTool(arg);
     else if (cmd.equals(RMTOOL))     doRemoveTool(arg);
     else if (cmd.equals(SENDBACK))   doSendCommand(arg);
     else if (cmd.equals(DEFMENU))    doDefineMenu(arg);
     else if (cmd.equals(MENUADD))    doMenuAdd(arg);
     else if (cmd.equals(MENURM))     doMenuRemove(arg);
     else if (cmd.equals(KILLMENU))   doDestroyMenu(arg);
     else showDebug("unknown command");
   }


   //
   // private methods
   //


   // generates a random string to be used as a key
   private String generateKey() {
     java.util.Random r = new java.util.Random();
     int i = r.nextInt();
     String s = String.valueOf(i);
     return s;
   }


   // browse to a url
   private void doBrowse(String url) {
     showDebug("doBrowse called with '" + url + "'");
     URL theURL = null;
     try {
       theURL = new URL(url);
     } catch (MalformedURLException e) {
       showDebug("exception: " + e);
```

```
      return;
    }
  mbApplet.getAppletContext().showDocument(theURL,
    mbTarget);
}


// audio operations
private void doPlayAudio(String url) {
  showDebug("doPlayAudio called with '" + url + "'");
  URL theURL = null;
  try {
    theURL = new URL(url);
  } catch (MalformedURLException e) {
    showDebug("exception: " + e);
    return;
  }
  mbApplet.play(theURL);
}

private void doLoopAudio(String url) {
  showDebug("doLoopAudio called with '" + url + "'");
  showDebug("not yet implemented!");
}

private void doStopLoop(String url) {
  showDebug("doStopLoop called with '" + url + "'");
  showDebug("not yet implemented!");
}


// toolbar operations
private void doAddTool(String toolSpec) {
  showDebug("doAddTool called with '" + toolSpec + "'");
  Words words = new Words(toolSpec);
  String name = words.nextWord();
  String command = words.remainingWords();
  if (name == null || command == null) {
    showDebug("invalid tool spec");
    return;
  }
  showDebug("tool: name=" + name + "; command=" + command);
  MBTool t = new MBTool(name, command);
```

```
      tools.addElement(t);
      updateToolbar();
   }

   private void doRemoveTool(String name) {
     showDebug("doRemoveTool called with '" + name + "'");
     for (int i = 0; i < tools.size(); i++) {
       MBTool t = (MBTool)tools.elementAt(i);
        if (t.getLabel().equals(name)) {
          showDebug("tool found and removed");
          tools.removeElementAt(i);
          updateToolbar();
          return;
        }
      }
     showDebug("tool not found");
   }

   private void updateToolbar() {
     showDebug("updateToolbar() called");
     if (toolbar == null) toolbar = new MBToolbar(this, tools);
     else toolbar.updateWith(tools);
     if (tools.size() > 0) toolbar.show();
     else toolbar.hide();
   }


   // login dialog
   private void doLogin() {
     showDebug("doLogin called");
     MBLoginDialog d = new MBLoginDialog(mbApplet.window);
   }


   // menu operations
   private void doDefineMenu(String arg) {
     showDebug("doDefineMenu called with " + arg);
     Words words = new Words(arg);   // <menuName> <cmdSyntax>
     //  [<item> ...]
     String name = words.nextWord();
     String items = words.remainingWords();
     if (name == null) showDebug("not enough words");
```

```
    else mbMenuBar.defineMenu(name, items);
}

private void doMenuAdd(String arg) {
  showDebug("doMenuAdd called with " + arg);
  Words words = new Words(arg);       // <menuName> <item> ...
  String name = words.nextWord();
  String items = words.remainingWords();
  if (name == null || items == null) showDebug("not enough
    words");
  else mbMenuBar.addItems(name, items);
}

private void doMenuRemove(String arg) {
  showDebug("doMenuRemove called with " + arg);
  Words words = new Words(arg);       // <menuName> <item> ...
  String name = words.nextWord();
  String items = words.remainingWords();
  if (name == null || items == null) showDebug("not enough
    words");
  else mbMenuBar.removeItems(name, items);
}

private void doDestroyMenu(String arg) {
  showDebug("doDestroyMenu called with " + arg);
  Words words = new Words(arg);       // <menuName>
  mbMenuBar.destroyMenu(words.nextWord());
}


//
// these are not private, so MBToolbar can find them
//

void doSendCommand(String command) {
  mbApplet.window.doSendCommand(command, true);
}

void doSendCommand(String command, boolean echo) {
  mbApplet.window.doSendCommand(command, echo);
}

// displays a general message about parsing status to the
//   console, if
```

```
      // MoonBean is in DEBUG mode.
      void showDebug(String s) {
        if (mbApplet.DEBUG) System.out.println("MBParser: " + s);
      }



} // class MBParser


// end of file MBParser.java, sick@butterfly.net
```

MBTextArea.java

```
/*
 * @(#)MBTextArea.java 1.0  06/07/96  sick@butterfly.net
 *
 * Copyright (c) 1996 HuskyLabs, Inc. All rights reserved.
 *
 */

/*

The MBTextArea class is used for the user display.

*/


package husky.mb;
import java.awt.TextArea;
import java.util.StringTokenizer;


/**
 * MBTextArea extends the basic TextArea by wrapping appended
 *    text to the
 * width (columns) of the text area.
 *
 * MBTextArea also trims the length of the text. This is a
 *    kludge because the
```

```
 * TextArea appears to 'fill up' at about 30k characters. This
 *    kludge is not
 * a perfect implementation; text trimming only occurs when
 *    appendText() is
 * caled, or trimText() is called explicitly.
 *
 * @version    1.0, 06/07/96
 * @author     Michael Reece <sick@butterfly.net>
 */
public class MBTextArea extends TextArea {

  /**
   * approximate maximum length, in characters, of the text.
   * @see #trimText
   */
  int trimAt = 15000;

  /**
   * approximate amount of text to remove, from the head of the
   *    string,
   * after the length has reached trimAt
   */
  int trimAmt = 5000;


  //
  // inherited constructors
  //

  public MBTextArea(){ super(); };
  public MBTextArea(String text){ super(text); };
  public MBTextArea(int rows, int cols){ super(rows, cols); };
  public MBTextArea(String text,int rows, int cols){ super
      (text, rows, cols); };


  //
  // inherited methods
  //


  /**
   * Appends the given text to the end, wrapping it to
   *    this.cols.
```

```java
 * @param str the text to wrap and append
 */
public void appendText(String str) {

  trimText();  // trim the TextArea text

  if (str.length() <= getColumns()) {
    // no need to wrap
    super.appendText(str);
    return;
  }

  StringTokenizer tokens = new StringTokenizer(str, " \t",
    true);
  String line = "";
  String next = "";

  while (tokens.hasMoreTokens()) {
    next = tokens.nextToken();
    if ( (line.length() + next.length()) > getColumns()) {
      // next token won't fit on this line, so append it
      super.appendText(line + "\n");
      // start a new line, prefixed by a single space
      line = (next.startsWith(" ")) ? next : " " + next;
    } else {
      line += next;
    }
  }
  super.appendText(line);
}

//
// new methods
//


/**
 * Appends the given text with a newline (\n) attached.
 * @see #appendText
 */
public void appendTextln(String str) {
  appendText(str + "\n");
}
```

```
/**
 * If the length of the text has surpassed trimAt, remove
 *    trimAmt
 * characters from the head of the text.
 */
public void trimText() {
  String t = getText();
  if (t.length() > trimAt) {
    // find the first \n after trimAmt, so we trim off clean
    // lines
    int amt = t.indexOf("\n", trimAmt);
    // and delete from 1..amt
    replaceText("", 1, amt);
  }
}


/**
 * Set the trimAt and trimAmt values.
 */
public void setTrim(int at, int amt) {
  trimAt = at;
  trimAmt = amt;
}


} // class MBTextArea


// end of file MBTextArea.java, sick@butterfly.net
```

MBLoginDialog.java

```
/*
 * @(#)MBLoginDialog.java  1.0  06/07/96  sick@butterfly.net
 *
 * Copyright (c) 1996 HuskyLabs, Inc. All rights reserved.
 *
 */
```

```
/*

MBLoginDialog.java contains the MBLoginDialog class.

*/


package husky.mb;


import java.awt.BorderLayout;
import java.awt.Button;
import java.awt.Dialog;
import java.awt.Event;
import java.awt.FlowLayout;
import java.awt.Font;
import java.awt.GridLayout;
import java.awt.Label;
import java.awt.Panel;
import java.awt.TextField;


/**
 * the login dialog box for MoonBean.
 */
class MBLoginDialog extends Dialog {

  TextField name = new TextField("");  // user name input
  TextField pwd = new TextField("");    // user password input
  MBWindow window; // parent window for modal dialog


  //
  // constructors
  //


  /**
   * constructor
   *
   * @param window the MBWindow to be used as the parent of the
   *    dialog
   */
```

```
public MBLoginDialog(MBWindow window) {
  super(window, "Login", true);
  this.window = window;
  Font f = new Font("System", Font.PLAIN, 13);
  if (f != null) setFont(f);

  Panel text = new Panel();
  text.setLayout(new GridLayout(7, 1, 0, 0));
  text.add(new Label("Welcome!"));
  text.add(new Label(""));
  text.add(new Label("To connect as a Tourist, simply click
    Login.  "));
  text.add(new Label(""));
  text.add(new Label("To connect as a Local, type your name
    and"));
  text.add(new Label("password below, then click Login."));
  text.add(new Label(""));

  Panel prompts = new Panel();
  prompts.setLayout(new GridLayout(2, 2, 0, 0));
    Panel u = new Panel();
    name = new TextField(20);
    u.add(new Label("Username"));
    u.add(name);
  prompts.add(u);
    Panel p = new Panel();
    pwd = new TextField(20);
    pwd.setEchoCharacter('*');
    p.add(new Label("Password"));
    p.add(pwd);
  prompts.add(p);

  Panel buttons = new Panel();
  buttons.setLayout(new FlowLayout(FlowLayout.CENTER, 25,
    25));
  buttons.add(new Button("Login"));

  setLayout(new BorderLayout());
  add("Center", prompts);
  add("South", buttons);
  add("North", text);

  pack();
  show();
```

```
        }


        //
        // inherited methods
        //


        /**
         * action method; responds to 'Login' button click
         */
        public boolean action(Event evt, Object arg) {
          String label = (String)arg;
          if (label.equals("Login")) {
            if (name.getText().equals("")) {
              window.doSendCommand("connect Guest CrabSoup", false);
            } else {
              window.doSendCommand("connect " + name.getText()
              + " " + pwd.getText(), false);
            }
          }
          this.hide();
          this.dispose();

          return true;
        }


    } // class MBLoginDialog


    // end of file MBLoginDialog.java, sick@butterfly.net
```

MBToolbar.java

```
/*
 * @(#)MBToolbar.java  1.0  06/07/96  sick@butterfly.net
 *
 * Copyright (c) 1996 HuskyLabs, Inc. All rights reserved.
 *
 */
```

```
/*
```

MBToolbar.java contains the MBToolbar and MBTool classes. MBToolbar is a frame that contains multiple MBTool objects. MBTool is a Button with a moo command attached.

```
*/


package husky.mb;


import java.awt.Button;       // GUI classes
import java.awt.Event;
import java.awt.Frame;
import java.awt.GridLayout;
import java.util.Vector;       // vector for tools


/**
 * the toolbar frame.
 */
class MBToolbar extends Frame {

  MBParser parent;  // the parser controlling this toolbar


  //
  // constructors
  //


  /**
   * constructor
   *
   * @param parser the MBParser controlling this toolbar
   * @param tools  the tools vector to be placed in the
   *    toolbar
   */
  public MBToolbar(MBParser parser, Vector tools) {
    super("Tools");
```

```
      this.parent = parser;

      updateWith(tools);
   }


   //
   // inherited methods
   //


   /**
    * action method; responds to tool button pushes by sending
    *    its attached
    * moo command.
    */
   public boolean action(Event e, Object arg) {
      String label = (String)arg;

      if (e.target instanceof MBTool) {
         parent.showDebug("toolbar push: " + arg);
         parent.doSendCommand(((MBTool)e.target).command);
      }

      return false;
   }


   //
   // new methods
   //


   /**
    * updates the toolbar with a new tools vector
    *
    * @param tools the new tools vector
    */
   public void updateWith(Vector tools) {
      int tnum = tools.size();

      int cols = 1;
```

```
    int rows = tnum;

    removeAll();

    setLayout(new GridLayout(rows, cols));
    for (int i=0; i < tnum; i ++) {
      add((MBTool)tools.elementAt(i));
    }
    pack();
  }


} // class MBToolbar



/**
 * a tool that fits in the toolbar. a MBTool is a Button with
 *    a moo command
 * attached.
 */
class MBTool extends Button {

  String command;  // the moo command



  //
  // constructors
  //


  /**
   * constructor
   *
   * @param label the label for this tool button
   * @param cmd   the moo command for this tool
   */
  public MBTool(String label, String cmd) {
    super(label);
    command = cmd;
  }
```

```
}   // class MBTool


// end of file MBToolbar.java, sick@butterfly.net
```

MBMenuBar.java

```
/*
 * @(#)MBMenuBar.java  1.0  06/07/96  sick@butterfly.net
 *
 * Copyright (c) 1996 HuskyLabs, Inc. All rights reserved.
 *
 */

/*

MBMenuBar.java contains the MBMenuBar and MBMenuItem classes.
Neither
class is declared public, and are only accessible within the
husky.mb
package.

*/


package husky.mb;


import husky.util.Words;    // "word" parser
import java.awt.MenuBar;    // menu classes
import java.awt.Menu;
import java.awt.MenuItem;


/**
 * MoonBean MenuBar, designed to work with MoonBean's protocol
 *    strings for
 * defining menus, menu items, and submenus.
 */
class MBMenuBar extends MenuBar {
```

```
/**
 * whether to show debugging info. debugging for the menu bar
 *    can be quite
 * verbose, so it has its own DEBUG flag rather than relying
 *    on
 * MoonBean.DEBUG for this.
 */
private final boolean DEBUG = true;



//
// inherited constructors
//


public MBMenuBar()  {  super();  }



//
// new methods
//


/**
 * defines a menu with the given name, syntax string, and an
 *    optional
 * list of initial menu items.
 *
 * @param name   the menu name
 * @param items a string of one or more "quoted items" to be
 *    a added to the
 *                menu. an item can be "label:command" pair or a
 *                "$sub-menu name$". if items is null, an empty
 *                menu is
 *                created.
 */
public void defineMenu(String name, String items) {
  showDebug("defineMenu: name=" + name + "; items=" + items);
  Menu menu = matchMenu(name);
  if (menu == null) {
```

```
      menu = new Menu(name);
      showDebug("adding new menu: " + menu);
      this.add(menu);
      if (name.equals("Help")) this.setHelpMenu(menu);
    } else {
      showDebug("removing items from " + menu);
      while (menu.countItems() > 0) menu.remove(0);
    }
    if (items != null) addItems(menu, items);
  }


  /**
   * add (or replace) a string of items to the named menu.
   *
   * @param name  the menu to add items to
   * @param items a string of one or more "quoted items" to be
   *     added to the
   *                 menu. items has the same syntax as for
   *                 defineMenu().
   */
  public void addItems(String name, String items) {
    Menu menu = matchMenu(name);
    if (menu != null) addItems(menu, items);
  }


  /**
   * remove a string of items from the named menu.
   *
   * @param name  the menu to remove items from.
   * @param items a string of one or more "quoted items" to be
   *     removed from
   *                 the menu. an item can be a "item label" to
   *                 remove an item
   *                 or "menu label" to remove a sub-menu.
   */
  public void removeItems(String name, String items) {
    Menu menu = matchMenu(name);
    if (menu != null) removeItems(menu, items);
  }
```

```
/**
 * removes the named menu or sub-menu.
 *
 * @param name the menu or sub-menu to be removed. name will
 *    be matched
 *                against any menu or sub-menu regardless of
 *                  nesting depth.
 */
public void destroyMenu(String name) {
  Menu menu = this.matchMenu(name);
  if (menu != null) menu.getParent().remove(menu);
}



//
// private methods
//


// remove items from the given menu
private void removeItems(Menu menu, String items) {
  showDebug("removing from " + menu + ": " + items);
  Words words = new Words(items);
  String item;
  while ((item = words.nextWord()) != null) {
    MenuItem mi = matchItem(menu, item);
    if (mi != null) menu.remove(mi);
  }
}


// add items to the given menu
private void addItems(Menu menu, String items) {
  showDebug("adding to " + menu + ": " + items);
  Words words = new Words(items);
  String item;
  while ((item = words.nextWord()) != null) {
    MenuItem mi;
    if (item.startsWith("$") && item.endsWith("$")) {
      // adding a $sub-menu$
      item = item.substring(1,item.length()-1);
      mi = new Menu(item);
      showDebug("created menu: " + mi);
```

```
      } else {
        // adding an item
        mi = new MBMenuItem(item);
        showDebug("created item: " + mi);
      }
      // see if it already exists
      MenuItem match = matchItem(menu, item);
      if (match == null || item.equals("-")) {
        // note "-" menu seperators are never 'replaced'
        showDebug("adding: " + mi);
        menu.add(mi);
      } else {
        showDebug("replacing: " + match);
        match = mi;
      }
    }
  }


  // match a menu on the menu bar or a nested submenu
  private Menu matchMenu(String name) {
    showDebug("matchMenu: " + name);
    for (int i = 0; i < this.countMenus(); i++) {
      Menu menu = this.getMenu(i);
      if (menu.getLabel().equals(name)) {
        showDebug("(match) returning menu " + menu);
        return menu;
      } else {
        MenuItem mi = matchItem(menu, name);
        if (mi instanceof Menu) return (Menu)mi;
      }
    }
    showDebug("matchMenu failed");
    return null;   // not found
  }


  // match an item on the given menu
  private MenuItem matchItem(Menu menu, String name) {
    int i = name.indexOf(":");
    if (i >= 0) name = name.substring(0,i);
    showDebug("matchItem: for " + name + " on " + menu);
    for (i = 0; i < menu.countItems(); i++) {
```

```
      MenuItem mi = menu.getItem(i);
      if (mi.getLabel().equals(name)) {
        showDebug("(match) returning item " + mi);
        return mi;
      }
    }
    return null;
  }


  /**
   * display debugging text if this.DEBUG is true
   * @param s the text to display
   */
  private void showDebug(String s) {
    if (this.DEBUG) System.out.println("MBMenuBar: " + s);
  }


}  // class MBMenuBar



/**
 * a menu item with a moo command attached
 */
class MBMenuItem extends MenuItem {

  /**
   * the moo command attached to this menu item
   */
  String command = "";


  //
  // constructors
  //


  /**
   * constructor; parses the label and command from a
   *   "label:command" pair
   *
```

```
 * @param label a label for a disabled item or "label:com
 *   mand" pair
 */
public MBMenuItem(String label) {
  super(label);
  int i = label.indexOf(":");
  if (i >= 0) {
    setLabel(label.substring(0, i));
    this.command = label.substring(i+1);
  }
  if (this.command.equals("")) this.disable();
}


//
// inherited methods
//


/**
 * the paramString() for this item, overridden to include
 *    this.command
 */
public String paramString() {
  return super.paramString() + "; command=" + this.command;
}


//
// new methods
//
/**
 * returns the command for this menu item
 * @retuns this.command
 */
public String getCommand() {
  return this.command;
}


} // class MBMenuItem

// end of file MBMenuBar.java, sick@butterfly.net
```

Words.java

```
/*
 * @(#)Words.java  1.0  06/07/96  sick@butterfly.net
 *
 * Copyright (c) 1996 HuskyLabs, Inc. All rights reserved.
 *
 */


package husky.util;


/**
 * parses a string into unquoted words or "quoted word groups"
 */
public class Words {

  String str = "";  // string to be parsed
  int idx = 0;       // current index


  //
  // constructors
  //


  /**
   * constructor
   *
   * @param s the string to be parsed
   */
  public Words(String s) {
    str = s;
  }


  //
  // new methods
  //


  /**
```

```
 * returns the next unquoted word or "quoted word group"
 */
public String nextWord() {
  while (idx < str.length()) {
    char ch = str.charAt(idx);
    if (ch == ' ') { // eat the space and keep advance
      idx++;
    } else if (ch == '\"') { // found a open-quote
      int i = str.indexOf('\"', idx+1);// look for close-
// quote
      if (i > -1) { // found close-quote
        String s = str.substring(idx+1, i); // return word
        // group
        idx = i + 1;
        return s;
      } else {                              // no close-quote
        String s = str.substring(idx);       // return what's
        // left
        idx = str.length();
        return s;
      }
    } else { // found an unquoted word
      int i = str.indexOf(' ', idx+1); // look for next space
      if (i > -1) {                           // found space
        String s = str.substring(idx, i);   // return word
        idx = i + 1;
        return s;
      } else {                               // no space
        String s = str.substring(idx); // return what's left
        idx = str.length();
        return s;
      }
    }
  }
  return null;  // no more words
}


/**
 * return the remaining words as a single string
 */
public String remainingWords() {
  return str.substring(idx).trim();
```

```
    }


}  // class Words


// end of file Words.java, sick@butterfly.net
```

## CHAPTER 26

Database Marketing

The Javanomics of Javatainment

Think about all the consumer goods in Circuit City or Sam's Club. They're probably stored, as objects, in a database somewhere. If you're a Sam's Club member, you're probably an object in that database, too. As you move through the store, collecting batteries, or large drums of capers, or flash-frozen filet of sole, you are not only filling your shopping cart and depleting your cash reserves, but you're creating a profile of yourself as a consumer. This profile is, in a sense, a persona in cyberspace. It is also more important to Sam Walton and his ilk than any particular item you might purchase, or even the items you might purchase over the course of your lifetime. Because in Sam's world, you do not exist. Only your persona does. The number on your card that is linked to the number on your checkbook that is linked to the number on your Discover Card (Sam's doesn't take Visa), which all goes back to your social security number, given to you at birth.

Media companies take your persona just as seriously. They need to market to you, to pitch you as a representative of your type to companies that hope to target their goods to you. Cyberspace communities are becoming as inundated with marketing messages as the broadcast spectrum. Advertising and direct marketing in one form or another is the economic backbone of the Internet. It is driving most new development. It is possible that microdenominations of e-cash allow for a viable economy of transaction-driven publications and entertainment. Or the online communities will have specific focuses, some educational institutions, some corporate business parks, others nightclubs and cafes. In the scope of human culture, economic exchanges are another form of discourse and communication. Money is digital and will become an integral part of cyberspace.

The current advertising and marketing paradigm is to generate "page impressions," hits, or "click-throughs" on the Web, which works as long as HTTP is the primary means of moving content around the Internet. As the Web warps around population clusters, and the users spend time interacting at a particular location, marketing will have to adapt from the banner-style ad to a more integrated approach. However things develop, the database is sure to become an ever more essential component. Let's look at how content is developed in a live collaborative environment, as opposed to the static Web. The new Webmaster, it appears, will be more commentator, game show host, bouncer and radio personality than engineer, administrator or architect.

CHAPTER 27   *Administrator, Engineer, Architect*

$bean_utils

To facilitate MOO programming that takes advantage of MoonBean protocol events, and to prevent misuse by restricting access, all messages are generated and transmitted by a MoonBean utilities object within the MOO, called $bean_utils. The $bean_utils is also responsible for keeping track of which users (also called 'players' in MOO) are connected via MoonBean and their secret 'keys' for preventing misuse. Trusted MOO programmers may access $bean_utils with the following verb calls.

display_url

Syntax:

display_url(who, url)

Displays the given URL to the the specified player.

Example:

```
$bean_utils:display_url(player, "http://www.butter
  fly.net/");
```

show_image

Syntax:

```
show_image(who, url)
```

Displays the image at the given URL. This is functionally equivalent to display_url(), but is provided as a seperate verb for clarity.

Example:

```
$bean_utils:show_image(player, "http://www.butter
  fly.net/sick/images/photo.jpg");
```

play_audio

Syntax:

```
play_audio(who, url)
```

Plays the audio clip at the given URL.

Example:

```
$bean_utils:play_audio(player, "http://www.butter
  fly.net/MoonBean/audio/moo.au");
```

loop_audio

Syntax:

```
loop_audio(who, url)
```

Begins looping the audio clip at the given URL.

Example:

```
$bean_utils:loop_audio(player, "http://www.butter
  fly.net/MoonBean/audio/soundtrack.au");
```

```
stop_audio
```

Syntax:

```
stop_audio(who, url)
```

Stops playing the audio clip.

Example:

```
$bean_utils:stop_audio(player, "http://www.butter
  fly.net/MoonBean/audio/soundtrack.au");
```

```
 add_tool
```

Syntax:

```
add_tool(who, label, command)
```

Adds a tool with the given label that responds with the given command.

Example:

```
$bean_utils:add_tool(player, "what's new", "news new");
```

```
remove_tool
```

Syntax:

```
remove_tool(who, label)
```

Removes the labeled item from the toolbar.

Example:

```
$bean_utils:remove_tool(player, "what's new");
```

```
define_menu
```

Syntax:

```
define_menu(who, label [, {item,cmd} | "-" | $submenu$
   ...])
```

Creates a new menu with the given label. Any existing menu with that name is replaced with the new menu. Optional arguments specify the initial menu items and/or sub-menus. A menu separator can be specified with a "-" argument.

Examples:

```
$bean_utils:define_menu(player, "Commands");
```

Creates a new menu labeled "Commands" with no items.

```
$bean_utils:define_menu(player, "Look", {"me","look
   me"}, {"room","look"}, "-", "$people$", "$things$");
```

Creates a new menu labeled "Look" with two items (me & room), a separator, and two sub-menus (people & things).

```
menu_additems
```

Syntax:

```
menu_additems(who, menu, {item,cmd} | $submenu$ [, ...])
```

Adds the specified items and/or sub-menus to the given menu.

Examples:

```
$bean_utils:menu_additems(player, "people",
  {"Sick","look ~Sick"}, {"KingCrab","look ~KingCrab"});
```

```
$bean_utils:menu_additems(player, "Commands", {"who's
  online","who"}, {"what's new","news new"});
```

```
menu_rmitems
```

Syntax:

```
menu_rmitems(who, menu, item [, ...])
```

Removes the specified items from the given menu. If <item> is the name of a sub-menu, the sub-menu will be removed.

Examples:

```
$bean_utils:menu_rmitems(player, "Commands", "what's
  new");
```

Removes the "what's new" item from the "Commands" menu.

```
$bean_utils:menu_rmitems(player, "Look", "things",
  "me");
```

Removes the "things" sub-menu and "me" item from the "Look" menu.

```
destroy_menu
```

Syntax:

```
destroy_menu(who, menu)
```

Removes the specified menu. \<menu\> can be a top-level menu or sub-menu.

Examples:

```
$bean_utils:destroy_menu(player, "Commands");

$bean_utils:destroy_menu(player, "people");
```

send_back

Syntax:

```
send_back(who, command)
```

Sends the given command back to the MOO as if it had been typed by the specified player.

Example:

```
$bean_utils:send_back(player, "go east");
```

Meet me on the Moon

Let's take a quick trip back to a MoonBean environment and look around.

```
http://www.lab.com/LiveJava/developers/ArtRoom.html
```

There are general instructions on how to operate your avatar within the MoonBean Web page. To test a MoonBean command, type *look me* in the terminal window. You should see a text description of your avatar in the MoonBean console and also see a graphic representation of your avatar in the browser. Now type *look here* in the terminal window. You should see the Art Room in the browser. If you press the buttons on the tool bar marked "self" or "room" you should get the same results.

The Art Room is an object on the MOO and a child of the Generic Trashable Room. To make the Art Room, I created an instance of a Generic Trashable Room. Java uses the term instance also. In Java, an object is an instance of a class. On the MOO, an object is an instance of its parent. The Generic Trashable Room is, in turn, a child of the generic room. When the Generic Trashable Room was first created, it was just another room, inheriting *properties* like Room.name, Room.description and Room.contents. In Java, properties are *instance variables*, or just *variables*. These properties can be changed for any particular instance of the room (such as the Generic Trashable Room or the Art Room or the Hot Tub as mentioned above; the Hot Tub is an example of a room) by using @rename and @describe.

@rename and @describe are examples of *verbs* on the MOO. A MOO verb is similar to a Java *method*. The verb alters the property in the same way that a Java method can affect a variable. To test this out, type in the terminal window:

```
@describe me as A brilliant programmer with a bowtie.
```

Now type *look me* or use the "self" button on the toolbar.

You will see that the verb altered the property, and **A brilliant programmer with a bowtie** appears in the terminal window. But the image is still the same in the browser. You look like a guest. So type:

```
@image_url me is http://www.lab.com/LiveJava/developer/
   prog.gif
```

Now look at yourself again.

The image in the browser should have changed.

And we'll perform one more experiment here. Type:

```
@icon_url me is http://www.lab.com/LiveJava/developer/
    bowtie.gif
```

Rather than looking at yourself, take a look at the room by typing *look here* or pressing the room button. The room has a property Room.contents that displays in the terminal window and in the browser the contents of the room. You can see that you are now represented by a bowtie in the room, and if you click on the bowtie, you get the room that was set as your home page. Any of these settings can be changed easily. Using a verb to change a property on one object (you), and thereby also changing a property of the room, illustrates the interaction of objects. In Java, this is analogous to methods interacting through messages to alter instance variables.

You should also be aware by now that two objects are interacting: you and the room. And that you are interacting through verbs, which are altering your properties. But there is more that can be done with this room in the context of the MOO as a whole. It can be made "fertile," which will allow any other MOO programmer to make an instance of the Art Room and continue the process afresh. For example, if you wanted to create a home for yourself called the Art Studio, that started with all the properties of the Art Room, but was extended with new verbs (in Java: *methods*) such as "paint" and "sculpt." Declaring a MOO object "fertile" is similar to declaring a Java class "public" but differs in important ways that will be discussed below.

Let's take a look at the output of some MOO commands that will show us how inheritance works. "Art" is a valid alias for the Art Room.

```
@parents Art
;The Art Room(#1178)    Generic Trashable Room(#856)
  generic room(#3)    Root Class(#1)
```

Since the Art Room is descended from the generic room, it has all the behaviors regarding exits and entrances and interior description that the parent class had. And because #1, the Root Class is in its ancestry, it has the fundamental built-in properties and verbs like a name, a description, and a way of looking at it (literally a verb named *look*).

To understand the concept of inheritance, let's take a trip back in time and visit the ancestors of the Art Room. Type: **@go #3**.

```
generic room
You see nothing special.
```

It doesn't look like much to the naked eye, but let's see what verbs are associated with this object (generic room). Type: **@verbs here**.

```
;verbs(#3) => {"confunc", "disfunc", "say", "emote",
  "announce", "match_exit", "add_exit", "tell_contents",
  "@exits", "look_self", "acceptable"
"add_entrance", "bless_for_entry", "@entrances", "go",
  "1*ook", "announce_all", "announce_all_but", "enter
  func", "exitfunc", "remove_exit", "remove_entrance",
  "@add-exit", "@add-entrance", "recycle", "e east w
  west s south n north ne northeast nw northwest se
  southeast sw southwest u up d down", "@eject @eject!
  @eject!!", "ejection_msg oejection_msg
  victim_ejection_msg", "accept_for_abode", "@resi
  dent*s", "match", "@remove-exit", "@remove-entrance",
  "moveto", "who_location_msg", "exits entrances",
  "obvious_exits", "here_huh",
  "room_announce*_all_but", "examine_commands_ok",
  "examine_key", "examine_contents", "tell_exits"}
```

This room, though not fleshed out, is really very featureful. It can be customized with entrances and exits, to display the contents of the room, to allow people inside to talk or express emotions or interact with other objects. Most importantly it gives the owner of the room rights to certain verbs that others don't have. For example, the owner of the room can use **@eject** on other people who happen to be in the room. This will move them to their home room.

Let's take a look at the source code of one of these verbs by typing: **@list here:tell_contents.** This verb, tell_contents, associated with this room (here) prints out the contents of the room when someone enters, when someone looks at it, or whenever the verb is called. Here is the output:

```
#3:"tell_contents"   this none this
 1:  contents = args[1];
 2:  ctype = args[2];
 3:  if (!this.dark && contents != {})
 4:    if (ctype == 0)
 5:      player:tell("Contents:");
 6:      for thing in (contents)
 7:        player:tell("   ", thing:title());
 8:      endfor
 9:    elseif (ctype == 1)
10:      for thing in (contents)
11:        if (is_player(thing))
12:          player:tell(thing:title(), " is here.");
13:        else
14:          player:tell("You see ", thing:title(), "
               here.");
15:        endif
16:      endfor
17:    elseif (ctype == 2)
18:      player:tell("You see ",
             $string_utils:title_list(contents), "
             here.");
19:    elseif (ctype == 3)
20:      players = things = {};
21:      for x in (contents)
22:        if (is_player(x))
23:          players = {@players, x};
24:        else
25:          things = {@things, x};
26:        endif
27:      endfor
29:        player:tell("You see ",
             $string_utils:title_list(things), " here.");
```

```
30:        endif
31:        if (players)
32:          player:tell($string_utils:title_listc
               (players), length(players) == 1 ? " is" | "
               are", " here.");
33:        endif
34:      endif
35:  endif
```

If you're not a programmer, this might seem overwhelming, but there are a few things that can be pointed out to get beyond the surface syntax into how this verb works. There are different types of objects on the MOO, players and objects they interact with, and they are handled differently by the tell_contents verb. Line 12 states that if the object is a player, the output statement will be "(players name) is here." If the object is not a player, but another type of object, the room will output "You see (name of thing) here" as stated in line 14.

It will be worth our while to step back and think about what we know so far of object-oriented programming. There are two objects here, you and the room. In Java, these objects would be instances of a class. Here on the MOO, they're just objects. In MOO, the objects have properties. In Java, they have variables. In MOO, the objects also have verbs, which can affect the objects' properties and cause the verbs of other objects to affect the properties of these other objects. In Java, the objects have methods that can affect the properties of that or other objects.

Just like we viewed the verbs associated with the room, you can see the verbs associated with you.

```
@verbs me
;verbs(#82) => {}
```

This doesn't mean that I don't have any verbs, but that there are no verbs unique to my object. I can still do things like look at the room, but that is because I inherited the ability to do this from my parents.

It's much easier for me, as a MOO character, to research by genealogy than it is in the outer world.

```
@parents me
motodave(#82)    generic programmer(#59)    generic
   builder(#4)    improved player(#98)    generic
   player(#6)    Root Class(#1)
```

It turns out that most of my abilities, or powers, or properties are derived from #59, the generic programmer. And a lot of them are derived from #4, the generic builder. When you first connect to most MOOs, there isn't very much you can do. You can't paste text from outside the MOO into the MOO terminal window (**@paste**), you can't join other players in other parts of the MOO (**@join**), you can't even use the verb **@verbs** to see what verbs are associated with a particular object. Generally, you need to change your heritage, something that is possible on MOOs but not possible in the outer world. To do this, you would type (don't actually do this, or you might wind up disabling your persona):

@chparent me to #98

But in the DogHouse, you don't need to do this, as every player is automatically descended from the improved player. The improved player was inserted into the lineage of all players, new and old, by changing the parent of the builder, the guests, and even the player to the improved player (**@chparent #4 to #98**). Interestingly, an object can become a descendant of its child.

As we can see above, looking on the verbs associated with the generic room object (#3), "look" is a verb that belongs to the generic room, which means it will work whenever you are in any room descended from the generic room. When you invoke "look" by typing "**look**" (or just "**l**" as look has a wildcard * after the l), the internal MOO parser first looks for a match for "look" on 'dobj' (direct object, the object that is looking, yourself), on 'iobj' (indirect object, the object that is looked at), then on the player's location. If you write a "look" verb on yourself, it will find that first, and if it doesn't find it on yourself or the object you're looking at, it'll find one on the room. If the verb isn't found, the MOO returns an "I don't understand that" message.

Here is the source code to the verb "look."

```
list here:look
#3:"l*ook"    any any any
 1:  if (dobjstr == "" && !prepstr)
 2:    this:look_self();
 3:  elseif (prepstr != "in" && prepstr != "on")
 4:    if (!dobjstr && prepstr == "at")
 5:      dobjstr = iobjstr;
 6:      iobjstr = "";
 7:    else
 8:      dobjstr = dobjstr + (prepstr && (dobjstr && " ")
          + prepstr);
 9:      dobjstr = dobjstr + (iobjstr && (dobjstr && " ")
          + iobjstr);
10:    endif
11:    dobj = this:match_object(dobjstr);
12:    if (!$command_utils:object_match_failed(dobj,
        dobjstr))
13:      dobj:look_self();
14:    endif
15:  elseif (!iobjstr)
16:    player:tell(verb, " ", prepstr, " what?");
17:  else
18:    iobj = this:match_object(iobjstr);
19:    if (!$command_utils:object_match_failed(iobj,
        iobjstr))
20:      if (dobjstr == "")
21:        iobj:look_self();
22:      elseif ((thing = iobj:match(dobjstr)) ==
          $failed_match)
23:        player:tell("I don't see any \"", dobjstr,
          "\" ", prepstr, " ", iobj.name, ".");
```

```
24:        elseif (thing == $ambiguous_match)
25:          player:tell("There are several things ",
                prepstr, " ", iobj.name, "one might call
                \"", dobjstr, "\".");
26:        else
27:          thing:look_self();
28:        endif
29:      endif
30:  endif
```

Understanding how the MOO finally works becomes a fairly mind-numbing proposition, as verbs reference other verbs, and all wind up making their way back to the Root object, #1. In Java, all objects are derived from java.lang.Object. Let's continue further though. I promise there's a payoff.

When you look at the room, line 13 of the "look" verb references the verb "look_self," which is owned by this room, as well as by the generic player and by the root. As mentioned, the version of "look_self" owned by the room is the one checked first.

```
@list here:look_self
#3:"look_self"   this none this
 1:  player:tell(this:title());
```

This tells the player the room's title (here:title, just returns this.name).

```
2:  if (!(args && args[1]))
3:    pass();
4:  endif
```

If there are arguments, and the argument is true, this will be skipped. Otherwise, pass() means "run the inherited :look_self." This does what #1:look_self normally does. The argument check comes into play when :look_self is called from :enterfunc(). If :enterfunc calls :look_self, it will pass the argument player.brief. If player.brief=1, then the if test in line 2 above will fail. this is 'brief mode' where you do not see the room's .description when you enter the room. Normally, player.brief=0 so you always see the description when you enter.

```
5:    if (this.tell_exits)
6:       this:tell_exits();
7:    endif
```

This calls :tell_exits() (@list here:tell_exits), which prints out the Exits: ... line.

```
8:    this:tell_contents(setremove(this:contents(),
         player), this.ctype);
```

This calls :tell_contents(), excluding the player from the objects to be displayed. It also passed this.ctype, which :tell_contents will interpret as the "format" to display the contents.

So, in English, "look" relies on "look_self" to find out what the room does when it is looked at. Each object has a :look_self that determines what happens when you look at that object. "Look_self" in turn relies on "tell_contents" to present the information about the objects in the room.

When you look at an object, you invoke **look_self** ($room:look_self or $player:look_self), depending on whether or not you are looking at a player or a room. This all goes back to #1:look_self. If none of the rules are fulfilled, the request is directed up the chain to the root. Thus, if you look at the generic room, you get a response "You see nothing special."

```
@list #1:look_self
#1:"look_self"    this none this
 1:    "... added for MoonBean support:";
 2:    url = this:image_url_msg();
 3:    if (url)
 4:       $bean_utils:browse_web(player, url);
 5:    endif
```

```
 6:   desc = this:description();
 7:   if (desc)
 8:     player:tell_lines(desc);
 9:   else
10:     player:tell("You see nothing special.");
11:   endif
```

Before we get too absorbed by the generic room and its capabilities, let's move forward in time to a descendant of the generic room, the Generic Trashable Room, #856. Type **@go #856**.

The Generic Trashable Room, and by extension the Art Room, has some verbs unique to it. Let's look at the Generic Trashable Room:

```
@verbs here
verbs(#856) => {"scrawl", "tell_contents", "trash",
  "spill", "tidy"}
```

It would look, at first glance, as if this is not a very featureful room, but in fact it has inherited all the verbs from its ancestor, the generic room. The verbs listed above are the ones that make it unique as the Generic Trashable Room.

The verb "trash", for example, allows people in the room to type "trash here with hot dog buns" and the result is that the phrase "hot dog buns" is added to a variable defined in the room (the variable is "junk"). But the "hot dog buns" are no good if they aren't immediately interactive, actually trashing the room.

To test it out type:

```
trash here with Coca-Cola
```

You immediately see on your screen:

```
Guest trashes The Generic Trashable Room with Coca-Cola.
```

To see the source code of the verb "trash," you can "list" the verb, associated with a particular object. The syntax is @list object:verb. Because you are in the object #856, you can type:

```
@list here:trash
```

and see the output:

```
#856:"trash"   this (with/using) any
     1:  junk = iobjstr;
     2:  mess = this.mess;
     3:  mess = setadd(mess, junk);
     4:  this.mess = mess;
     5:  this:announce_all(player.name, " trashes ",
            this.name, " with ", junk, ".");
```

To see more effects of your trashing of the room, look at the room again by typing: **look here**. Depending on when you visit and who is in the room, the output will be slightly different.

```
Generic Trashable Room
A brightly lit public bathroom.
The place has been trashed with hot dog buns, food, and
  Coca-Cola.
There are Pabst Blue Ribbon spills all over the floor.
Scrawled on the wall, you see: Spinoza was right.
You see Golf Club here.
Guest, Sick, Obvious, and motodave are here.
```

There is a version of "tell_contents" that is unique to this room. As we noted, the MOO looks for the verb on the local room first before working its way back through the lineage looking for a match. When you look at the Generic Trashable Room, "look" calls "look_self" which in turn calls "tell_contents." From our discussion of OO programming, you will see the benefit of developing full, stand-alone solutions that work in different contexts with minor adjustments. Here is the code for the Generic Trashable Room's version of "tell_contents."

```
command:
@list here:tell_contents
```

```
Response:
#856:"tell_contents"    this none this
 1:   if (length(this.mess) != 0)
 2:     player:tell("The place has been trashed with ",
            $string_utils:english_list(this.mess), ".");
 3:   endif
 4:   if (length(this.spillage) != 0)
 5:     player:tell("There are ",
            $string_utils:english_list(this.spillage),
            "spills all over the floor.");
 6:   endif
 7:   if (length(this.grafitti) != 0)
 8:     player:tell("Scrawled on the wall, you see: ",
            $string_utils:english_list(this.grafitti),
            ".");
 9:   endif
10:   pass(@args);
```

The first line (1) says that if the length of the property is nonzero (if there is actually a mess) then the verb prints out the type of mess (spillage, graffito or trash) and the string describing the stuff that the room was trashed with.

The last line (10) says "now go up into the parents and look for a verb also called "tell_contents" and run that too." You can see that the room used the version of "tell_contents" cited above to display the other inhabitants of the room (Obvious, Sick, guest and motodave) and the Golf Club.

Join the Golf Club

CCP bridges the gap from a text-based database object in the MOO to a full-fledged hypermedia incarnation in cyberspace. Pick up the golf club (in the CrabHouse it's object number #225). I'll leave one in the Art Room for you.

```
@examine golf
Golf Club (#225) is owned by Obvious (#139).
(No description set.)
Obvious Verbs:
  whack <anything> with #225
  g*et/t*ake #225
  d*rop/th*row #225
  gi*ve/ha*nd #225 to <anything>
```

It is pretty simple object by most standards. It has the basic verbs inherited from its parent, the generic thing (#5), and the only addition is that it can "whack" someone. What happens when you whack another player?

```
whack Obvious with golf
motodave brains Obvious with a Golf Club.
```

The verb seems pretty simple. It's announced to the room that Obvious was brained. Now try it on yourself. You'll see that more is communicated than just the text-based whack. Abuse is hurled from across the Web and displayed in the browser of the victim. Now we get out beyond the "links," into an immersive environment that spans cyberspace.

```
@list golf:whack
#225:"whack"   any (with/using) this
 1:  player.location:announce_all(player.name, " brains
       ", dobj.name, " with a ", this.name, ".");
 2:  $bean_utils:browse_web(dobj, "http://www.xe.com/
       cgi-bin/nph-abuse");
```

The first line is the text-based announcement. The second line utilizes the MoonBean protocol to direct the victim's browser to fetch a URL from anywhere on the Web. $bean_utils is a MOO utilities object, an object that houses a collection of related utility verbs. The $bean_utils object provides an easy and consistent manner for communicating to MoonBean, to invoke actions such as browsing we b pages, or playing audio files by tying together a MOO action with an HTTP transaction. The end result can be a well-designed cyberspace in which to live.

Technical Terms
and Additional Resources

To keep the resources current as new books are released, Web sites come online and terms are coined, I have made the bibliography and glossary interactive. Please feel free to send suggestions to the author (motodave@butterfly.net).

http://www.lab.com/LiveJava/terms.html

http://www.lab.com/LiveJava/resources.html

Index